# DESPERATE
*for*
# GOD

CROSSWAY BOOKS
BY NANCIE CARMICHAEL

*Your Life, God's Home*

*Desperate for God*

# DESPERATE

*for*

# GOD

HOW HE MEETS US
WHEN WE PRAY

NANCIE CARMICHAEL

CROSSWAY BOOKS • WHEATON, ILLINOIS
A DIVISION OF GOOD NEWS PUBLISHERS

**Library of Congress Cataloging-in-Publication Data**
Carmichael, Nancie.
    Desperate for God : how he meets us when we pray /
Nancie Carmichael.
      p.   cm.
    ISBN 1-58134-089-3 (hc : alk. paper)
    1. Prayer—Christianity. I. Title.
BV210. 2.C335  1999
248.3'2—dc21
                                            99-23343
                                            CIP

| 15 | 14 | 13 | 12 | 11 | 10 | 09 | 08 | 07 | 06 | 05 | 04 | 03 | 02 | 01 | 00 | 99 |
|----|----|----|----|----|----|----|----|----|----|----|----|----|----|----|----|----|
| 15 | 14 | 13 | 12 | 11 | 10 | 9 | 8 | 7 | 6 | 5 | 4 | 3 | 2 | 1 | | |

*Blessed be God,*

*Who has not turned away my prayer,*

*Nor His mercy from me!*

PSALM 66:20 NKJV

# CONTENTS

# Acknowledgments

Special thanks to the wonderful people at Crossway—to Ebeth and Lane Dennis for their commitment to publish Christian literature, to Marvin Padgett for his editorial direction and encouragement and especially for his prayers, to Brian Ondracek for his creative direction, to Kathy Jacobs for her assistance in helping me get the word out, to Lila Bishop for her excellent editing skills. *Thank you!*

I will be forever indebted to the special people in my life who have been my prayer mentors. My life is transformed because of their prayers: Mother and Dad, Gunder and Harriet Pearson, now in His presence; my mother-in-law and father-in-law, Betty and Harold Carmichael, who pray daily for their large extended family and circle of friends; Earl and Dorothy Book, an extraordinary couple who live in a spirit of prayer. And I am blessed beyond measure to be married to Bill, a praying husband and father.

Jerome, one of the early church fathers, wrote: "The toil my writing cost me, the difficulties I underwent, how often I gave up in despair, and how I started again, both I who knew the burden and those who lived with me can bear witness." (Me too, Jerome!)

I am so grateful to those who "live with me"—my husband, Bill, and children Jon, Brittni, and Will; Eric; Chris; Andy, and Amy—and for the love and patience they extend to their "writing" wife and mother. "There is no greater joy than to know your children walk in truth. I thank God every day for you and as others have prayed for me, I will pray for you always!"

# $\mathcal{I}$NTRODUCTION

*Prayer is not another part for us to act, another skill for us to master. . . . It is a relationship, a relationship with God.*[1]

SIMON TUGWELL

In the hallway of our home are four prints of Thomas Cole's *Journey of Life*. They capture in a dramatic way the four stages of life—infancy, youth, midlife, and maturity. Every day I walk past the artist's portrayal of the stages of life, and every day I am reminded that our life with God, too, is a journey filled with passages, much like our physical lives. Our prayers reflect those passages.

I grew up in a home with praying parents. I have been surrounded and covered by prayer and have always known that praying is a good thing to do. And yet for all the talk about prayer, what did I really know of it? Some time ago at a grocery check-out stand, a *Life* magazine featuring prayer caught my eye, and I put it with my purchases. The cover was a beautiful, serene face of a child, hands folded, eyes upraised in faith. The boy who was bagging my groceries stopped and held the magazine, critically appraising the cover. "I'm so sure that's what I look like when I pray! It's more like this." He grabbed his hair and exclaimed, "HELP!"

I laughed and admitted that has been my experience, too. Prayers are often "emergency flares" I shoot up to God, but I'm finding that prayer is much more than that. I still feel like a kindergartner in this area, and yet I'm seeing that prayer is like walking into a room with a door that leads into another room—with a door that leads into another room.

That's because prayer is about relationship with God, and relationships are not static. They are either growing or cooling off. Think of it: Relationship with the almighty God, creator of heaven and earth, the one who gave His life for me and cares intimately about the details of my life. It is an awesome concept.

Grace Brame wrote, "Holiness is not a state to be gained by going away from life, but by entering into it in the most vital way, especially through prayer—the prayer of adoration, the prayer of communion that we share with others, intercessory prayer, and life lived as a prayer of love. . . . Although some are truly called to a contemplative vocation, all of us are called to prayer in the midst of ordinary life."[2]

I understand now what I didn't understand years ago—that the closer I get to God, the more ordinary I will be. Prayer is very ordinary, very common to life, and connects us with God. And yet it has taken me many years to really begin to take prayer seriously. Early on in my life, I somehow had the idea that prayer—real prayer—was for other people, not me. It was for those who were "called" to be intercessors or who lived a more cloistered, spiritual life.

When I was a girl, I would stay in town with my grandmother on Saturdays so I could have my piano lesson. The walk to my teacher's house took me past a convent, and I would slow my steps, secretly intrigued by the sisters praying in the chapel. My Grandma Olson, a practical no-nonsense woman who'd raised four children alone in the Depression, was not impressed. "You can't be so heavenly minded you're no earthly good," she said.

I thought wistfully that if someone wanted to be a person of prayer, she had to be sort of holy, mystical—certainly she would not wear blue jeans and ride bikes and laugh a lot, which I liked to do— and still do! But even then my heart yearned after Him, aware of the God-shaped vacuum that only He could fill, the Living Water that alone quenches the thirst.

When I was young, I prayed to accept Jesus as my Savior, and now and then I would shoot up quick prayers, especially when I was in trouble. I received a jolt one morning when, as a freshman in college, I came to class ill-prepared for the test the professor was handing out. Then he had the nerve to pray, "Lord, bring to remembrance what each student has studied." I needed him to pray for a miracle for me to know the answers! It began to occur to me that God is more than a genie in a bottle.

It was when I was a young mother with a toddler and a new baby that I tentatively tried the door of prayer. My husband, Bill, had taken a new job as a youth pastor, and I felt very alone and over my head with added parenting and church responsibilities. One Sunday evening in church as I sat in the back cradling my little ones, I offered up this simple prayer: "Yes." All I could do, I told God, was offer myself to Him just as I was—a person filled with self-doubt and anxiety.

Over the years I've prayed this prayer many times. Sometimes the prayer sticks in my throat. Sometimes I pray it with fresh urgency. But with that step, I began to understand: Prayer is being available to God. An astounding concept—to think that He calls me His beloved, and I dare to call Him my Friend; to know that this relationship can deepen through the years to take me to more effective prayers and a more effective life for Him.

I think so often of Jesus' two friends Mary and Martha. Mary was the one who sat at His feet, while Martha rushed about serving (Luke 10). I tend to identify with Martha, as the "Grandma Olson" in me tells I should do something, and I find it hard to wait. After all, I rationalize, prayer can be as practical as asking for daily bread, even though Jesus clearly said that Mary was the one who had her priorities straight.

A young woman came up to me after I had spoken about prayer. "I know what you're saying is true," she said. "There are desperate needs, and we do need to pray. And yet is that all we should do? It doesn't seem enough to just pray." I told her that indeed it is our sense of helplessness that drives us to prayer. Prayer must be the beginning place of all doing, where in our helplessness we realize that God is all we can hold onto. And that is where He meets us. As long as we are self-sufficient, we don't need Him.

As Bill and I drove home some time ago from speaking at a family conference on how to have healthy families, we were struck by the devastated young husband who told us his wife was leaving him and their two small children. His story was not that much different from many others we'd heard. On the drive home, we felt as if we'd waded through a major battlefield, dispensing Band-Aids and aspirin when situations called for intensive care. How could we tell this young man, "Just follow these six easy steps, and all will be well"?

Not long after this, Bill and I began to hold "prayer summits" for families. We found that although we families need sound teaching and helpful information, some problems today are too desperate, too complex for an easy response. In our prayer summits, we simply offer a time in which we pray for families. We have seen answers to prayer. We've also noticed that after the prayer summits, there seems to be a tangible difference among people—a sense of empowerment, of strength and peace. What happened? We were the same people with the same needs, but in the humility of asking and coming to an all-powerful God, we were changed. In prayer, He changes us.

Scripture says to "pray without ceasing," and though often we are aware of God's presence, some days His absence is all that we feel. But it's all right to feel helpless and desperate before God. Andrew Murray wrote, "Never forget the two foundational truths on which this blessed waiting rests: thy absolute helplessness; the absolute sufficiency of thy God."[3] Desperation is what drives us into His presence, and we can come to Him, the one who redeems and restores.

The reason I have written this book is that I am increasingly aware of the need for prayer. But our prayers—like us—change from time to time and reflect where we are with God. Why do we hear so much now on prayer?

## THE DESPERATE TIMES CALL US TO PRAYER

*The end of all things is near. Therefore be clear minded and self-controlled so that you can pray.*

1 PETER 4:7

These truly are desperate times. What fuels desperation? Fear. What cures desperation? Love. As Scripture reminds us, "Perfect love casts out fear." Prayer makes a difference—and desperate prayers are powerful. During some of my speaking assignments, I have been taking surveys about prayer. Out of over three hundred surveys, 99 percent of the respondents said they had seen direct answers to their prayers. Nearly all wrote of desperate times in their lives when God met them—times when they were turned inside out over drug and alcohol problems with their children, divorce, deaths, serious illness, or a job loss. They needed prayer!

But prayer can be a mystery, too. Over half said there were times when it didn't seem that their prayers were getting through to God, and they wondered if He'd forgotten them. Many struggled with finding the time and place to pray. But all of them were convinced there was something powerful in prayer and wanted to see their prayer lives grow.

Can our prayer lives grow? Yes. The wonderful thing about our life in God is that we always have an opportunity to grow and learn more about Him. We also have the option of not growing—of living a limited spiritual life. It is up to us. God is there. We just need to draw near to Him.

Our prayer lives reflect our journey with God—growth charts, if you will. Each of the four sections of this book will focus on a specific aspect of growth—infancy, youth, midlife, maturity. In each of these phases, we are driven to Him by desperation, by fear. In infancy, it is the fear of abandonment. In youth, it is the fear of not having a purpose. In midlife, it can be the unexpected storms of life. And in maturity (or old age), the fears that linger are like those of infancy—the fear of being alone and forgotten.

At times in this journey of life we operate under the illusion that we are at a stopping place, especially in the consuming stages of youth and young adulthood. And yet we are always changing. There are places in our lives that offer us the opportunity to go on to the next step, to grow. At times we miss these opportunities, but God is faithful, and He will help us grow if we will only listen. It is as if we are on a conveyer belt, and even if we do not seem to be changing at the moment, things around us are.

We are conditioned to solve problems and to move on. But sometimes we feel stuck, trapped. And perhaps the most difficult things to bear in our lives are the chronic, nagging problems that hang on. But then most of life is unfinished business, and for that we must thank God for His mercy. Unfinished means that there is the possibility of better things. There is hope. Relationships, finances, careers, children—all of these unfinished works in progress have potential for improvement or for redeeming. We need His intervention. We need Him! And He does meet us.

The goal in prayer is to learn to come simply, as a child. The desperation of a child who knows his Abba, Father, has behind his cry confidence—that the Father will hear and respond. It is a prayer that leads to peace and relinquishment, as Jesus taught us to pray: "Thy kingdom come; Thy will be done."

The good news is that along with the desperation of the times, sweeping throughout the world is a pervading sense that we must pray. I'm encouraged to think that even by the act of my writing about prayer and your interest in reading a book on prayer, you have already begun to pray. Your intention to draw near to God is part of your prayer, as well as your commitment of time and money to focus your attention to hear what He has to say to you. You have made an appointment with God—a very clear sign of your intention. You are making an important investment.

Prayer brings us to God, but we come with different degrees of desperation. Because we're all different and at different stages of growth, we all approach prayer differently. One person's prayer is not necessarily more spiritual than another's. Only you and God know the obvious and the not-so-obvious needs of your life, but how blessed you are when you know your need of Him. This is the beginning place of prayer.

> Let us pursue the knowledge of the Lord. His going forth is estab-
> lished as the morning; He will come to us like the rain, like the
> latter and former rain to the earth.
>
> HOSEA 6:3 NKJV

We all come to prayer with a tangled mass of motives— altruistic and selfish, merciful and hateful, loving and bitter.

Frankly, this side of eternity we will never unravel the good from the bad, the pure from the impure. But what I have come to see is that God is big enough to receive us with all our mixture. We do not have to be bright, or pure, or filled with faith, or anything. That is what grace means, and not only are we saved by grace, but we live by it as well. And we pray by it.[4]

RICHARD FOSTER

## HOW TO USE THIS BOOK

- Read it thoughtfully. Take time to reflect on where you are in your prayer life.

- Determine to start where you are, now.

- Above all, be honest with God. Invite Him into the deepest, darkest places of your heart. Lay before Him the things you cannot bear to speak of to anyone else. Pour out your soul before Him. For God to meet your most desperate needs, you must be honest about them.

- Carve out a place—an actual, physical place—where you pray. Take time to respond to the questions in the back of each section of this book and write them in your prayer journal. (If you're like me and travel a lot, your "place" may be a tattered spiral notebook, which you keep with your Bible, where you write your prayers.) Your "place" may be a certain time of day.

- Incorporate Bible reading and praise with your prayers, because it will help establish faith and help you know whom you're praying to. It will also help reveal your own heart.

↶ Have your own prayer summit with God. Meet with two or three friends who will commit to pray. Dare to pray believing for answers. Pray for others who need Jesus. "The fervent prayer of a righteous person avails much" (James 5:16 NKJV).

# *I*NFANCY

## DESPERATION OF AN INFANT
## NEEDING ITS PARENT

⁂

*God, I feel so alone. Sometimes it seems impossible to go on. There are times I cry out to You, but I don't know if You're listening—or even there. Yet something pulls me, draws me. I know You are there, but I am desperate to really know it—to know that You are involved in my life.*

*Lord, I guess I am crying out for You to hold me. A simple reaching up of my faith to You, the Abba Father who promised never to leave me nor forsake me.*

*I come to You, Lord—terrified and scared—in need of the basics, in need of my daily bread, and I come to You because You are my Father. Forgive me for trying to get everything figured out first. Our Father in heaven, hallowed be Your name. Amen.*

⁂

For you did not receive a spirit that makes you a slave again to fear, but you received the Spirit of sonship [or adoption]. And by him we cry, "Abba, Father." The Spirit himself testifies with our spirit that we are God's children.

ROMANS 8:15-16 NIV

# One

## WHAT DO
## I NEED?

❧

*The questions that matter in life are remarkably few, and they are all answered by the words—"Come unto Me." Not—do this, or don't do that; but—"Come unto Me."*[1]

OSWALD CHAMBERS

❧

Babies are such a great way to start people!

The first painting of Thomas Cole's *Journey of Life* shows a beautiful baby in the dawn of a new day floating serenely down a gentle river with angels flitting around. One thing I've noticed about babies though—they don't need a handbook on how to get their needs met, as my husband, Bill, and I were reminded last week when we babysat our nineteen-month-old grandson.

Although Will's vocabulary is limited, he managed to communicate his needs very well—needs his Papa and I were more than eager to meet! Will is just beginning to talk and uses little one-word sentences: "Book. Nana. Juice. Cup." As adorable as these little words are, it is Will's arms reaching out to me and his smiles of pleasure when he gets the cracker he wants that makes me scoop him up in my arms. He is irresistible!

Beginning prayer is like that. We turn to Him, our words poor, stumbling. But when we turn our whole hearts to Him, calling out with our desperate needs, knowing He is all-powerful and loving, knowing He will meet us, He does. We simply come to Him believing that He is. *And we are irresistible to Him.* He says, "Come to Me, all you who labor and are heavy laden, and I will give you rest" (Matt. 11:28 NKJV).

Tiny children are honest about their needs. They feel hunger and thirst. They get tired; they need comfort and rest. And they soon learn where to go to get their needs met—to their parents. So it is with prayer. We tend to get all lofty and complicated about prayer, but our Father says, "What do you need? Come. Ask. Seek. Knock."

We may think we have to pray a certain way, forgetting that prayer is just the vehicle to take us where the power is—to our Creator—the one who made us and shapes our lives, the one who can meet our needs.

It's like using the telephone. It would be silly for me to lavish time and attention on the telephone itself, instead of just seeing it as an instrument I need to keep in working order so I can communicate, connect with people. Prayer is the instrument to connect with God. We may think we have to pray using certain words or learn eloquent ways of expressing something. We don't. We must be simple, honest, direct. Anne Lamott, in *Traveling Mercies,* tells of an acquaintance who prays in the morning, "Whatever," and in the evening, "Oh, well." A lot can be said in a few words if our hearts are in them.

I believe this simplicity is what Jesus had in mind when He said, "Assuredly, I say to you, unless you are converted and become as little children, you will by no means enter the kingdom of heaven. Therefore whoever humbles himself as this little child is the greatest in the kingdom of heaven. Whoever receives one little child like this in My name receives Me" (Matt. 18:3-5 NKJV).

## IT'S IMPORTANT TO KNOW OUR NEEDS

> Need comes not from discovering Christ's all-sufficiency; it comes from stumbling upon our insufficiency. But in this self-congratulating day in which we've come to live, we've congratulated ourselves completely out of spiritual neediness. It is rarely possible to save the "un-needy," since honesty and need are what bring us to Christ in the first place. . . . Spiritual need is rooted in our honesty.[2]

CALVIN MILLER

## DOES GOD REALLY WANT TO HEAR FROM ME?

Look deeply and honestly within yourself. What do you need? We must know what we need in order to ask. It's essential to be honest in our prayers, knowing that when we pray, we are calling out to God, to our Abba Father.

Children are so refreshingly *there*—simply in the moment. They are not wishing or dreaming for another place and time. They are acutely aware of their basic needs, and they call out to their parents for those needs to be met, knowing there will be a response. That is faith, and Hebrews 11:6 says that is how we are to approach God: "But without faith it is impossible to please Him, for he who comes to God must believe that He is, and that He is a rewarder of those who diligently seek Him" (NKJV).

In our beginning spiritual experience, we have definite needs: The need to know He is there, the need to know Him, the need for a refuge, the need to know we are just beginning the greatest adventure of all time.

It is my opinion that we should never completely know ourselves unless we seek to know God. It is by gazing at His Majesty that we get in touch with our own lowliness. It is by looking at His purity that we shall see our own faith. It is by pondering His humility, that we shall see how far we are from being humble.[3]

TERESA OF AVILA

~ *1* ~

# I NEED TO KNOW
# HE IS THERE.

*But You, O Lord, do not be far from Me;*
*O My Strength, hasten to help Me!*

PSALM 22:19 NKJV

God is always with us. Prayer is simply being aware of Him with us.

When I was very young, I remember going on a trip with a family I did not know well, and we stayed for several days in a place I'd never been before. They left me at the home of another family while they visited some other people they knew. I'm sure it was a nice family, but I vividly recall being desperately homesick. Nothing could make the aching void go away until I was again with my mother and dad. And the instant I was home again, I was fine. The only cure for homesickness and fear is to be with the ones you are missing and love so much.

A. W. Tozer wrote:

> Fear is the painful emotion that arises at the thought that we may be harmed or made to suffer. This fear persists while we are subject to the will of someone who does not desire our well-being. The moment we come under the protection of one of good will, fear is cast out. A child lost in a crowded store is full of fear because it sees the strangers around it as enemies. In its mother's arms a moment later all the terror subsides. The known good will of the mother casts out fear . . . to know that

love is of God and to enter into the secret place leaning upon the arm of the Beloved—this and only this can cast out fear.[4]

I was ten years old when my brother Joe was born. His presence in our home was a delight to me, and I considered my good-natured little towheaded brother my personal property as I helped my mother care for him. One day after my mother put Joe down for a nap, I watched as she puttered about picking things up, straightening his room. She confided to me in a whisper, "He's not asleep yet, but he likes knowing that I'm near."

Indeed he did, and soon relaxed into a deep sleep. There is nothing like the primary relationship between an infant and the parent. Exhausting, yes, and all-consuming, but there is no doubt of the bond of love. A young woman told me of her deep struggles with rejection in her past. During prayer she "climbed up" into God's lap—a new concept for her—but as she prayed in the arms of her Abba Father, she sensed God's comfort and acceptance, as well as an awareness of things she needed to confess. She told me it was a fresh beginning of *knowing* God's love.

*Oh, to know that He is near.* It is the beginning place of prayer, the desire to draw near. To simply know He is there, that He cares. One of the names of our Lord, *Jehovah-Shammah,* means "The Lord Is There." The name is a figurative reference to Jerusalem during the millennial reign of Christ, portraying an intimate, caring, involved, and "in-charge" Lord. It is the Abba Father relationship that makes us want to run to Him like a child, to be held by Him. I believe this is the beginning place of prayer—the desire *to know He is near.* It is a primal, urgent need.

Our yellow lab Sam loves being near me. I have no idea why, but I think it's because I'm the one who's home most of the time, and if he gets fed and walked and petted, it's often from me. I'm the one who takes care of his basic needs. He's not my dog, you understand—he belongs to my daughter Amy—but since she's at school most of the time, here we are. Sam is the one with whom I talk through some finer points of theology, because he is always at my feet as I sit at the computer. He has no agenda other than hanging out with me, and nothing delights him more than when I put on my walking shoes and jacket and get the leash. He becomes ecstatic with joy. But until then, he follows me from room to room, contented just to be there.

I can learn a lot from Sam about entering into the simple delight of knowing that my heavenly Father is near, knowing He will meet all my needs according to His riches in glory.

> *For as high as the heavens are above the earth,*
> *so great is his love for those who fear him;*
> *As far as the east is from the west,*
> *so far has he removed our transgressions from us.*
> *As a father has compassion on his children,*
> *so the Lord has compassion on those who fear him.*

PSALM 103:11-13

*Prayer*
*Lord, am I honest about my needs,*
*and do I present them to You?*

## ~ 2 ~

## I Need to Know
## Who He Is.

*How precious is Your lovingkindness, O God!*
*Therefore the children of men put their trust*
*under the shadow of Your wings.*
*They are abundantly satisfied with the fullness of Your house,*
*And You give them drink from the river of Your pleasures.*
*For with You is the fountain of life; In Your light we see light.*

PSALM 36:7-9 NKJV

A friend told us of a time when he visited church with his grand-mother. In the Sunday school class, they asked him to pray. He panicked, for the only thing he knew of prayer was what he'd seen on *Little House on the Prairie*. When they prayed, they bowed their heads and folded their hands. So he did that and then counted under his breath slowly to thirty. He knew about prayer, but he didn't know the one to whom he was supposed to be praying.

When we come to know God through the Word, we grow. Reading the Bible is important in growing in our prayer life, because Scripture tells us whom we're praying to. I think it's impossible to grow in prayer without growing in the study of God's Word.

Reading the Bible not only shows me Christ; it increases my faith, as Romans 10:17 says, "Faith comes from hearing the message, and the message is heard through the word of Christ." Prayers of faith are powerful. There are lots of people praying to many gods. There's a lot of fuzzy stuff out there, spiritually speaking. But to really *know Him* is to know the God of the Bible.

Besides, our earthly fathers influence our concept of the heavenly Father, and some of us need to have that concept redeemed and corrected by the Word. Psalm 86:15 says this about the character of God: "But you, O Lord, are a compassionate and gracious God, slow to anger, abounding in love and faithfulness."

A. W. Tozer wrote, "If you would follow on to know the Lord, come at once to the open Bible expecting it to speak to you. Do not come with the notion that it is a thing which you may push around at your convenience. It is more than a thing; it is a voice, a word, the very Word of the Living God."[5]

My earliest memory of prayer was being led into it, as my father often had what we called "family prayer." We would gather around and pray. If one of us was sick, Dad and Mom would kneel at the bedside, lay their hands on the sick child, and pray.

Once when I was a very small girl, I watched my mother sweeping the kitchen floor, as she did every day. Sweeping the floor was no idle exercise on the farm in Montana with kids and pets and men with boots walking in and out. Mother stopped right in the middle of sweeping, leaned upon her broom with a pile of dust in the middle of the floor, and began to pray most earnestly.

I don't remember whom she was praying for, only that she prayed. I'm sure my mother was unaware of my watching and listening. It was so natural, just a part of the day for her. This was not unusual for my mother, who frequently would pray for someone. Perhaps it was one of her relatives with whom she often got together and then would be "burdened" for, because the person didn't know the Lord.

So I grew up seeing that prayer was natural, heartfelt. Prayer was often accompanied by agony and tears and at other times with praise and rejoicing. Prayer was personal, and it was global. We prayed for all the missionaries we knew, for family members near and far, for our church, and for our nation.

But when did I first pray? It's one thing to be surrounded by prayer; it's quite another to pray from one's own heart. For many years I relied on the prayers of my parents, although I was quick to offer up prayers before a test or for protection or for guidance. It was later, after I'd left home and gone to college and I had my own "desperation" times, that I began to realize how much I needed to pray. I knew where to turn because I'd seen it modeled.

*Prayer*
*Lord, do I know who You are from Your Word?*
*Do I know Your character, Your personality?*

~ *3* ~

## I Need to Know He Wants Relationship with Me.

*Oh, that I knew where I might find Him,*
*That I might come to His seat!*
*I would present my case before Him,*
*And fill my mouth with arguments.*
*I would know the words which He would answer me,*
*And understand what He would say to me.*
*Would He contend with me in His great power?*
*No! But He would take note of me.*

JOB 23:3-6 NKJV

Not only is beginning prayer the awareness that He is near—but that He takes *note* of me. He *notices me*—and wants to have relationship with *me*. That truth is hard to take in. I have seen an illustration of this through birth.

Birth is an amazing miracle, as it brings us a new relationship. Our newest family member is our first little grandson, Will, whose birth was truly one of the nicest things ever to happen to our son Jon, his wife Brittni, and our entire family. To have relationship with this wonderful little guy is a priceless gift—and do we ever "notice" him! It will probably be good for Bill and me to have other grandchildren so Will doesn't get too much "noticing!"

But relationships take care. I read somewhere an unknown author's comment: "We are born naked, wet and hungry. Then things get worse." Yes, babies are adorable, but they're helpless and need a lot of attention. But even though they have many needs, we're more than willing to meet them because the relationship is so precious. Our hearts are captured—we're in love.

There are many people today who want to pray, who want relationship with their heavenly Father, but they're not sure how that can happen. In order to have a relationship with God, we must be born again—a love relationship must happen.

Where is the beginning place of spiritual birth? It begins with desire. And desire begins with need—with an awareness that we need to be born again, that we need His resurrection power to live in this world. Don't be afraid of need, because that is where, when we cry out to Him, "Lord, be merciful to me, a sinner," He comes to us.

All of us have experienced physical birth. Someone gave birth that we might have life. Some of us also experienced the miracle of adoption. Bill and I have been privileged to go through four birth experiences with our sons and an adoption experience with our daughter. Birth is necessary for life. Christ also gave us birth—new spiritual birth, and there are obvious parallels between physical birth and spiritual birth.

LABOR AND PAIN

One week before our first son, Jon, was born, I got to church on Sunday and gratefully sank into the pew. As I looked at my feet, I was horrified to see that I had on two different shoes—a navy blue and a brown one. I couldn't see my feet until I sat down! Bill and I collapsed in giggles and then sneaked up to the balcony for church.

At this point, I felt as if I would be pregnant forever. The idea of giving birth was scary. I told my sister, "It's impossible! I cannot do this. I want this baby, but I'd like to skip the labor part of it." She comforted me by saying, "The next time you're in a big crowd, look around you and remember that everyone you see was born. It *is* possible." And sure enough, it was.

Birth stories are wonderful, and we all have them. But we know that birth can be painful. It does require labor. It can be messy. It can create all kinds of panic. It can be inconvenient. In adoption, too, there is the not-knowing, the waiting, the agony. But the labor, the tears, the pain, the indignities are forgotten in the joy of the new life.

Jesus went through incredible agony and pain to bring us life so that we could have a relationship with Him. In Gethsemane he prayed, "Let this cup pass from me." What He faced must have seemed daunting. He knew it would be agony—having the sin of the world placed on Him so the Father couldn't even look upon Him then. There would be physical torture, horrible pain. But He prayed, "Not My will, but Yours." And Hebrews says, "Jesus . . . for the joy that was set before Him endured the cross" (Heb. 12:2 NKJV). Jesus said, "For this cause I was born" (John 18:37 NKJV).

## FRESH AWARENESS OF THE MIRACLE OF LIFE

Being a parent is simply an unfolding mystery and wonder to me, and it is certainly humbling. Birth is an amazing miracle—the child growing within. I have tucked in my Bible in Psalm 139 a sonogram of our grandson, Will, as a reminder that God forms us even there within the womb.

When we participate in the amazing life force of birth, we try to understand and cooperate with it. Yet we can't help realize that we are simply participants in something huge, so vast—knowing there has to be a Creator at work.

To the natural mind, the "new birth"—becoming a child of God through His Son Jesus Christ and believing that we can have relationship with Him and communicate with Him—staggers the mind. In John chapter 3, Nicodemus—a thinker—asked Jesus, "How can this be?" Jesus said, "You must be born again." Nicodemus, incredulous, asked sarcastically, "Oh, go back to my mother's womb and be born again?"

How does the new birth happen, being born of the Spirit? It is, simply put, a miracle. A holy mystery. Romans 5:1-2, 8 says, "Therefore, since we have been justified through faith, we have peace with God through our Lord Jesus Christ, through whom we have gained access by faith into this grace in which we now stand. . . . But God demonstrates his own love for us in this: While we were still sinners, Christ died for us." Being born again means we can have relationship by the same faith that Abraham, David, the disciples, Paul,

St. Augustine, Martin Luther, Teresa of Avila placed in God. You and me. All of us down through time.

Just as the miracle of physical birth staggers my mind, so does the miracle of the spiritual rebirth. Yet as with physical birth, we submit to the spiritual new birth in obedience through the truth of the Word, and we begin the faith walk, learning to communicate with Him as we go. Also we become participants in a vast faith venture alongside other believers.

### NEW PRIORITIES

Birth is not something you just fit into your day-timer. It takes precedence. Everything else pales before it. It changes everything. A new baby is a new relationship and forever changes the family dynamics. There's someone new now to love, to know, to care for. Everything is turned upside down! I have vivid memories of riding home from the hospital with Bill with each new baby, somehow seeing the trees, the street on which I lived, our house with new eyes. Things were irrevocably changed by each new birth.

When we follow Christ, we have new priorities. Second Corinthians 5:17 says, "If anyone is in Christ, he is a new creation; the old has gone, the new has come!" He turns everything in our lives upside down! We don't fit Him into our day-timer, as everything pales before knowing Him as Lord. We become aware that we are part of a wonderful family—with a loving, good Father at the head, with Jesus Christ the Cornerstone, and with the Holy Spirit as guide and counselor. Often we are afraid of giving all to Christ—perhaps afraid of losing control. But He says, "Come to me, all you who are weary and burdened, and I will give you rest. Take my yoke upon you and learn from me. . . . For my yoke is easy and my burden is light."

The prophet Isaiah tells us that Jesus was born *to us*—given *to us*. And His name? Wonderful, Counselor, the Mighty God, the Prince of Peace, the Everlasting Father. And all that you need, He will be to you.

## REAL LOVE, REAL JOY

You can't help it; your heart is captured—even in the middle of the night when you're completely sleep-deprived and you hear that piercing little cry and know it's time for a feeding. You poke your husband with your toe, and he pokes you, because after all, you're nursing. So you stumble toward the crib, longing for the good old days when you slept all night. Then you see a little face smiling at you, loving you, reaching up to you—and you melt! You can't help it. You're in love.

God loves us that way, only with a more perfect love, and longs for us to talk to Him, to have relationship. This is the beginning place of prayer. He longs for us to turn to Him that He may heal us, comfort us, meet our needs. He wept over Jerusalem: "O Jerusalem, Jerusalem . . . how often I have longed to gather your children together, as a hen gathers her chicks under her wings, but you were not willing" (Matt. 23:37).

We aren't a pain to Him. We aren't an unplanned birth. We're not an inconvenience—even when we cry out in the middle of the night with our oh-so-human needs. The Lord said through His prophet Isaiah,

"Can a mother forget the baby at her breast and have no compassion on the child she has borne? Though she may forget, I will not forget you! See, I have engraved you on the palms of my hands" (49:15-16).

He comes, leaning over us, loving us, caring for us. He says, "I have come that they may have life, and have it to the full" (John 10:10). And as we stay in relationship with Him, we grow. "Like newborn babies," 1 Peter 2:2 says, "crave pure spiritual milk, so that by it you may grow up in your salvation, now that you have tasted that the Lord is good."

*Prayer*
*Lord, is it really possible that You gave Your life so that*
*I might have a relationship with the Almighty One?*

*The Lord your God is with you, he is mighty to save. He will take great delight in you, he will quiet you with his love, he will rejoice over you with singing.*

ZEPHANIAH 3:17

~ *4* ~

## I NEED TO KNOW THAT
## HE IS A REFUGE FOR ME.

*Keep me safe, O God, for in you I take refuge.*
*I said to the Lord, "You are my Lord;*
*Apart from you I have no good thing."*

PSALM 16:1-2

When our son Eric was a toddler, we went to a shopping center at Easter time. There was a giant bunny handing out candy to children. Eric's big brother, three-year-old Jon, was delighted, but Eric was terrified. He scrambled up on my lap, saying, "No way!" He didn't know many words, but he didn't like the looks of that creature and took refuge in my arms.

Eric's a tall, strapping young man now—over six-foot-four. But like all of us, he knows the world can be scary. However, we can take refuge in God. Psalm 32:6-7 says, "Therefore let everyone who is godly pray to you while you may be found; surely when the mighty waters rise, they will not reach him. You are my hiding place; you will protect me from trouble and surround me with songs of deliverance."

And because He is our refuge, we can hide *in Him*—not *from Him*—when we are in right relationship with Him. In the Garden of Eden, Adam and Eve hid from God after they had sinned. Sometimes we dread honesty because the truth about ourselves is just too painful, unbearable. But we don't need to hide from God, to fear being honest with Him, for when we come openly to Him—no defenses, no covering up—He will meet us. He longs for a relationship with each of us and waits for us to come to Him just as we are. He wants to heal us, cleanse us, and restore us. As I read through the Bible, over and over I am impressed by the fact that whenever people came to God—even with tentative steps—He met them more than halfway. He is not a vindictive God; He is a loving Father who longs for His children to turn to Him for their safekeeping.

Sue Stanley went through a series of devastating losses. Her parents died in the spring of 1990 in a murder-suicide. A year later her husband left her. Within a short period of time, she was an orphan and a single mom, trying to comfort her children in their losses as well. She was not sure how she could go on, but she told me how God met her in (of all places) a movie theater.

Her son Brian was four, and she was taking him to the movies for the first time, going with her neighbors. On the way the neighbor's all-knowing five-year-old daughter told Brian that theaters were dark, and he probably wouldn't like it. They got there, bought their tickets, and were laden with popcorn and treats when Brian balked. Everyone else had gone in, but Brian stood at the door and wailed, "No, no, no!"

Sue tells me that as she leaned down to talk to her sobbing son, the Lord whispered in a still, small voice, "Sue, what you are going to say to Brian, I am saying to you."

She found herself saying, "Honey, I know it's dark in there, and I know you're scared, but I brought you here because I know something you don't know. I've been here before, and I know what it's like in there. There's something really good in there, and I know you'll like it, but you can't see it unless you go in."

Sue said as she was speaking, she immediately thought of Jeremiah 29:11: "I know the plans I have for you, plans to prosper you and not to harm you." She continued, "I'm not sending you in there alone. I'll be with you and hold your hand, and I won't let go." She thought of Isaiah 41:10: "So do not fear, for I am with you; do not be dismayed, for I am your God. I will strengthen you and help you; I will uphold you with my righteous right hand."

Sue said Brian grew calmer and was listening to her. She then had a further inspiration. She poked her head into the dark theater, came back, and said, "Brian, it's only dark in this little hallway. Around the corner there are little lights on the floor, lights on the walls, and lots more light from the screen." She knew she was talking about the little lights in her life—the strategic people God had sent as comforters and advisers, who brought her joy and laughter in the midst of unbelievable pain. And the best light of all—Jesus Himself: "The Lord is my light and my salvation!"

Finally convinced, Brian looked up at his mother, took her hand, tucked his popcorn under one arm, and walked into the theater with her. When they sat down next to their friends, Sue's neighbor asked where they'd been. All Sue could manage was, "I just had an encounter with the living God in the lobby!"

Sue looks back on that seemingly ordinary day as a defining moment when she *knew* that in the most desperately dark time of her life, God was her refuge.

Brennan Manning asks, "Do you really accept the message that God is head over heels in love with you? I believe that this question is at the core of our ability to mature and grow spiritually. If in our hearts we really don't believe that God loves us as we are, if we are still tainted by the lie that we can do something to make God love us more, we are rejecting the message of the cross."[6]

Early childhood experiences shape our attitudes toward prayer. Honest prayer can be threatening, because when we are honest about our lives, we can't help but see our desperate needs. Honesty promotes humility. But we can feel safe with Him because He sees us—His children—with such love. Why should it be so difficult to be His child, to just accept His grace and love?

> Avoid being bashful with God. A fine humility it would be if I had the Emperor of Heaven and Earth in my house, coming to it to do me a favor and to delight in my company, and I were so humble that I would not answer His questions, nor remain with Him, nor accept what He gave me, and I were so humble that I preferred to remain poor and even let Him go away, so that He would see I had not sufficient resolution. Have nothing to do with that kind of humility.[7]
>
> TERESA OF AVILA

> I have been driven many times to my knees by the overwhelming conviction that I had nowhere else to go. My own wisdom and that of all about me seemed insufficient for the day.[8]
>
> ABRAHAM LINCOLN

*"Because he loves me," says the Lord,*
*"I will rescue him; I will protect him,*
*for he acknowledges my name.*
*He will call upon me, and I will answer him;*
*I will be with him in trouble, I will deliver him*
*and honor him."*

PSALM 91:14-15

*Prayer*
*Lord, do I truly make You my refuge,*
*and do I run into Your name as a strong tower of deliverance?*

~ *5* ~

PRAYER:
PROFOUND YET ORDINARY

*When You said, "Seek My face,"*
*My heart said to You, "Your face, Lord, I will seek."*

PSALM 27:8 NKJV

The Bible often refers to our prayers as fragrance. Revelation 5:8 describes golden bowls of incense at the altar in front of the Almighty, filled with the prayers of His people. Consider all of the prayers that have been prayed and are being prayed all over the world. Many profound prayers have been written over the centuries. There are reams of books on how to pray. We have prayer breakfasts, national days of prayer, prayer seminars. And yet prayer is very personal, very individual.

I love fragrances, preferring bath oils and lotions, which tend to be more subtle than perfume. My mother used to like English lavender. I still have some of her things in the back of my closet, and now and then I'll bury my nose in her sweater, trying to remember the essence of *her.* Fragrance is very individual, and we may not even be aware of our own distinctiveness. My son's friend Darrin used to say when he was little and came to our house that our house had a certain "Carmichael" smell. I'm not sure what that was, maybe a combination of things— cooking, soaps or detergents. (I do hope it was a good smell!)

When my children were very small and used to play outside on a windswept spring afternoon, they came in with a fragrance that was *them*. It was reminiscent of sun and wind and dirt and new leaves. We—God's children—are a fragrance to Him. And if I know anything about God from the pages of the Bible, it is that, yes, He longs to hear from us, His children. Yes, a thousand times yes! Maybe our fragrance isn't always so "wholesome," but it is *us!*

Each of my children is unique and wonderful, and whenever I hear from any of them, I am overjoyed. When I get homesick for our grandbaby, I'll call Jon and Brittni just to hear Will speak a word or two over the phone (or just do heavy breathing!), and I'm delighted to hear even that.

I think that's how God regards our communication with Him. We come as children, pouring out to Him the essence of who we are—confessing our sin, our weakness. And as we grow to know Him more, our prayers take on different dimensions. But primarily, it is important to be very simple, very honest in prayer, calling out to Him from who and where we are, believing that He hears us. C. S. Lewis wrote, "We must lay before Him what is in us, not what ought to be in us."[9]

God welcomes my prayers and your prayers as we tumble them up to Him—an essence of us, His children. We are, according to 2 Corinthians 2:15, "to God the fragrance of Christ among those who are being saved and among those who are perishing."

One day last spring, we were having a family prayer time as we were all going separate directions. Amy was getting ready to go on a music tour to California, and her cat Spooky was very sick. We were all distressed over it, especially Amy. Spooky was old, but he was like a member of the family. So when it was my turn to pray, I began to pray for Spooky, which got a giggle or two out of a couple of the kids: "Lord, You said that You care about the birds that fall, so surely you care about Spooky." I think they were laughing because Spooky had killed more than his share of birds. (In fact, our son Chris accused Spooky of being a serial bird killer.) We all ended up laughing in that prayer, but we cried, too, because we loved that old cat. And he did die.

The thing is, God cares about the most intimate details of our lives. There is no "sacred and secular." What do we think? That God only tunes in to us when we have long, somber expressions on our faces and use a stained-glass voice? No! Of course we come when our children cry, but we love it when they laugh, too. At times some resist prayer, possibly because they see prayer as "911"—or as a last resort, irrelevant to ordinary, common life.

What relief to know that God is even in the mundane details of our lives, that He has compassion on our humanity. Eberhard Arnold wrote, "A person must be converted twice; once from the natural to the spiritual, and then again from the spiritual to the natural."[10]

> *I cried out to God with my voice—*
> *To God with my voice; and He gave ear to me.*
>
> PSALM 77:1 NKJV

We are not beggars on the one hand or spiritual customers on the other; we are God's children, and we just stay before Him with our broken treasures or our pain and watch Him mend or heal in such a way that we understand Him better. If we are asking God to give us experiences, we hurt the Lord. The very questions we ask hurt Jesus because they are not the questions of a child.[11]

OSWALD CHAMBERS

*Prayer*
*Lord, it's wonderful to know I don't have*
*to be profound or eloquent. Just being with You*
*in the midst of my life is enough!*

~ *6* ~

## PRAYER:
## GUIDANCE FROM HIS EYES

*I will instruct you and teach you in the way you should go;*
*I will guide you with My eye.*

PSALM 32:8 NKJV

The bonding time for adoption—especially if the child is older—can take some time and special attention. When our Amy came to us at age three, I wasn't sure how to connect with her. She had spent the first three years of her life receiving minimal care in an orphanage in Korea. I had no idea of the depth of rejection that an abandoned child experiences on a gut level. Often I felt helpless to know how to convince her of my love, and it was difficult getting through to her. But as I prayed, it seemed that God urged me to "nourish her with my eyes." So I tried to give her lots of smiling, warm eye contact—looks of approval and acceptance, and it did seem to help.

A parent's warm gaze of approval and love is a powerful bond. After the recent birth of our grandson, Will, he lay quietly, his eyes wide open. As we gazed back at him, it seemed we could see forever into his dark blue eyes. We covered him with kisses. "Who are you, most wonderful child? We are so glad you are here. We love you so much!" Whenever I am with Will, I never tire of looking at him, of memorizing every detail of him. Even now when Bill and I are with Will—our joyful toddler—we can't take our eyes off him. He is such a delight.

It astounds me to think that we are created for God's pleasure (Rev. 4:11) and that just as we delight in looking at our children and grandchildren, He is delighted in us. Indeed, He can't take His eyes off us! Scripture says, "He guides us with His eye," as we turn to Him with our simple, heartfelt prayers. Like Amy, who needed extra nourishing with a parent's loving eye contact, we who were in the "far country" of sin need to be near Him—to look upon Him, knowing He loves us. Basking in His gaze—this, too, is prayer.

How good to know that "the tabernacle of God is with men, and He will dwell with them, and they shall be His people. God Himself will be with them and be their God" (Rev. 21:3 NKJV).

> There is no need to talk a lot in prayer, but stretch out your hands often and say, "Lord, as you want and as you know, have mercy on me." But if there is war in your soul, add, "Help me." And because he knows what we need, he shows us his mercy.[12]
>
> MACARIUS THE ELDER (OF EGYPT)

*Come, let us bow down in worship,*
*let us kneel before the Lord our Maker;*
*for he is our God and we are the people of his pasture,*
*the flock under his care.*
*Today, if you hear his voice, do not harden your hearts.*

PSALM 95:6-8

*Prayer*
*Lord, am I resting in the knowledge that*
*You are guiding me, nourishing me with Your loving gaze?*

~ *7* ~

## PRAISE:
## PRAYERS GROWING UP

*Out of the mouth of babes and nursing infants You have*
*    ordained strength. . . .*
*O Lord, our Lord, how excellent is Your name in all the earth!*
*I will praise You, O Lord, with my whole heart;*
*I will tell of all Your marvelous works.*

PSALMS 8:2, 9—9:1 NKJV

Praise and gratitude don't come naturally for most of us. These prac-
tices are a discipline. Some of the very first words we teach our children to say are "thank you" and "please." Gratitude is not naturally in
us, but is a quality we must cultivate and train into our children and
into our prayer lives as well. Fallen creatures that we are, our minds
tend to think negatively and tend toward fear, to think we deserve
whatever we have coming to us. But in our growing walk with God,
right from the start we must learn not only to petition Him but to
thank Him. It's only polite, because, after all, the very air that we
breathe is a gift from Him. Our lives are gifts from Him. The food that
we eat, the water that we drink are from Him.

Henry Ward Beecher wrote:

So many are God's kindnesses to us, that, as drops of water,
they run together; and it is not until we are borne up by the
multitude of them, as by streams in deep channels, that we

recognize them as coming from him. We have walked amid his mercies as in a forest where we are tangled among ten thousand growths and touched on every hand by leaves and buds which we notice not. We cannot recall all the things he has done for us. There are so many.[13]

How quickly we assume that all good things are our right. Colossians 3:1-2 tells us to set our mind on things that are above, not on things of earth. To "set" means that it takes a conscious effort to praise, to think the good, to be grateful.

Childhood is wonderful, but we can't stay there. To be healthy, we must grow. It is one thing to stay "childlike" in our approach to God, but we should not be childish. Baby talk is cute when you're small but not so cute as you grow up. First Corinthians 13:11 says, "When I was a child, I spoke as a child, I understood as a child, I thought as a child; but when I became a man, I put away childish things" (NKJV). Yes, God is here to meet our basic needs, but it is His plan that we grow in our faith in Him. Catherine Marshall wrote, "Praise is faith in action."[14]

We are all called to prayer. We begin where we are and then grow by giving God praise and honor, loving and serving those He places in our lives. Eventually we must grow beyond the idea that God is here to *serve us*, beyond the idea that God is simply the source of energy for carrying on *our* activities. That is why prayer is so important. And so *difficult,* because prayer confronts us with who we are; and *prayer leads us to God.* It would be easier to write on other things, such as self-esteem or marriage or raising children—all of which Bill and I teach sessions on and believe are extremely important. But these are not the principal thing—prayer is.

We become very good at avoiding the most personal, painful issues, the most pivotal issues. We can be very creative at avoiding *Him.* For instance, even in writing this book, from time to time I realize I am writing about prayer, rather than praying about what I must write. Then I must stop and incline my heart again to Him and come as a child again to my Father.

Prayer pulls us to the real agenda. Prayer is getting beneath the surface: *Am I His follower?* If God is real, it must be the most important fact in my life. Am I taking the time to sit at His feet—to know Him? "Martha, Martha, you are worried and troubled about many things. But one thing is needed," Jesus said (Luke 10:41-42 NKJV). It's much easier to discuss the peripherals, more comfortable, and they, too, are part of life—all necessary and good. But the heart of the Gospel, Jesus reminds us, is sitting at His feet, communicating with Him, offering up a sacrifice of praise to Him.

Yes, God wants to hear from us, His children. But more than that, we need to hear from Him through knowing He is there and through resting in His presence. We know Him by trusting Him and honestly asking Him for our needs. We hear Him through knowing who He is by reading the Bible. And our trust and confidence in Him grow through knowing Him more fully by praising Him and thanking Him for the answers to our prayers and just for who He is.

Why pray? Because you're His child, and He values you just for who you are. He has much to show you. When we first come to Him, it is only the beginning of understanding and knowing Him through prayer—a journey that will take us on the greatest adventure of our lives.

*Prayer*
*Lord, do I remember to praise You often*
*for Your wonderful blessings?*

Instead of grateful recognition of unworthiness to receive the gifts of God, there is so often acceptance without gratitude or contrition but with complaint when things go wrong. Though there is no single evidence by which to discern a Christian, there is an index by which one may test his own experience. Confronted by pain and annoyance, does one say, "Why does this have to happen to me?" Or encompassed by God's bounties, does one say, "Who am I that I should be thus blest?"[15]

GEORGIA HARKNESS

*Prayer of Praise*

*Lord, I praise You for Your presence. Thank You for Your Word that says as we praise You, Your presence comes, and in Your presence is fullness of joy. I praise You that I can "run into Your name" and that You are a refuge and a high tower for me. You keep me safe and sheltered in Your presence.*

*I praise You for life, for the very air I breathe, for the food I eat, for each morning in which You offer Your mercies, new again. I gratefully accept them, knowing I need to keep close to You, Father, because I want to have Your image stamped on my life so that others around me will know I am Your child. I rest in You, Lord. Amen.*

WAYS TO GROW:

LEARNING HOW TO COME AS A CHILD

꙳ Remember, we are all at different places spiritually, as in "age." Some of us have known the Lord a long time. Some of us are new at living the Christian life. Maybe some of us are not on good speaking terms with God, but regardless of where you are, determine to come as a child.

꙳ Decide upon a certain length of "quiet time"—perhaps fifteen, twenty minutes, maybe more—and have a designated place if possible. If you can, go outside. See the stars or the wind in the trees; see the sky. *Be still.* Think about His majesty, His faithfulness. Find a verse or two in the book of Psalms to read as a praise, and when you're ready, read the psalm as a prayer, meaning it with all your heart.

꙳ Ask yourself the following questions, taking time to write them in your prayer journal. After you honestly answer them for yourself, pray them to Him, writing your prayers if you wish:

1. Am I truly His? Think about the concept of spiritual birth. Have you accepted God's gift of new life that you may be rightly related to Him? To become His children, we must be born again, a holy mystery. Read John 3; Romans 5; 10:8-10; Psalm 51.

2. Am I growing to know Jesus? Study a young child you may know and consider how he relates to his parent. Pray for insight on what it means for you to approach God as your

Abba Father. It takes study and time to know His real character, His true nature. Ephesians 4:14-15 encourages us to grow up in Him.

3.  What are my needs, and am I presenting them honestly to God? Do my prayers make me sound more like one of God's customers than one of His children? Philippians 4:19 says, "And my God will meet all your needs according to his glorious riches in Christ Jesus. To our God and Father be glory for ever and ever. Amen."

꙳ Do I remember to praise Him for the answers? Philippians 4:6 says, "Do not be anxious about anything, but in everything, by prayer and petition, with thanksgiving, present your requests to God."

꙳ As David Needham writes in *Close to His Majesty,* remember that "all He is, He is to me." Search out and meditate upon Scriptures that minister to you at your deepest point of need and praise God for His provision. (Psalm 139; Isaiah 40; Matthew 5, 6, and 7 are especially comforting.)

These, then, are the four rich sources of prayer. Out of contrition for sin is supplication born. Prayer comes of the fidelity to praises and the fulfillment of what we have undertaken for the sake of a pure conscience. Pleading comes forth from the warmth of our love. Thanksgiving is generated by the contemplation of God's goodness and greatness and faithfulness. And all this, as we know, often evokes the most fervent and fiery prayers.[16]

JOHN CASSIAN

*To be with God wondering, that is adoration.*
*To be with God gratefully, that is thanksgiving.*
*To be with God ashamed, that is confession.*
*To be with God, with others on your heart,*
  *that is intercession.*

UNKNOWN

*Reflections*

_____

_____

_____

_____

_____

_____

_____

_____

_____

_____

_____

_____

_____

_____

_____

_____

_____

_____

_____

_____

_____

_____

*Reflections*

# $\mathscr{Y}$OUTH

## DESPERATION OF A YOUTH
## SEEKING A PURPOSE

*Father, I do want to be used by You. Sometimes I'm not sure what my purpose is in life, and so many things call to me. There are so many things I "want." I am hungry for life, Lord, hungry for experience, for challenge. But may I not be led into temptation; instead, make me hungry for more of You.*

*Capture my heart, Lord! If I am not in You, I cannot stand in this world. The pleasures and gifts the world offers are such illusions; they are so temporary. May I never grow tired of praying to know Your purpose and will and of pursuing a joyous and ever-expanding relationship with You.*

*I'm aware that I have only one life to live here on earth. Show me, Lord, how to honor You with my life. May Your will be done on earth as it is in heaven. Amen.*

Then I heard the voice of the Lord saying, "Whom shall I send? And who will go for us?" And I said, "Here am I. Send me!"

ISAIAH 6:8

# *Two*

# WHAT IS
# MY PASSION?

⋙

*[David speaking] For who is this uncircumcised Philistine, that he
should defy the armies of the living God? . . . Is there not a cause?*

1 SAMUEL 17:26, 29 NKJV

⋙

The second painting of Thomas Cole's series titled the *Journey of Life*
depicts the idealism of youth. The young man is steering his boat
down a river, and up ahead are endless possibilities. There are billowing clouds and castles in the sky, and the expression on his face is
eager. I know that expression well.

In parenting our five children, Bill and I have had a teenager in our
house for *sixteen continuous years*, as our youngest, Amy, is now a
junior in high school. And when we were first married thirty years
ago, we were youth pastors, so it seems we've always been surrounded
by young people. There is something very wonderful about them.
Sometimes they are maddening, but we love their infectious passion
for life, their dreams and hopes. Life is full of highs and lows, laughter and dreams, hope and despair. Anything seems possible, and
sometimes nothing seems possible.

They are passionate about their loves, their sports, and even their food. As my son said the other day, "I *love* pizza!" His comment reminded me about a youth group that was serving pizza at a youth function, and there was a sign over the pizza that read: "Take only two pieces. God is watching." At the other end of the table, one of the kids put up another sign: "Take all the cookies you want. God is watching the pizza!"

Life is so vivid at this place—so on the edge. It's interesting to note that many love stories about teenagers are concerned with the tragedy of death and unrequited love—*Romeo and Juliet* in all its variations, *Westside Story,* and *Titanic.* Perhaps these stories capture the imagination because you're not ready to live until you're ready to die. And being young is definitely a time to live, although there are many dangers along with the opportunities. The dangers, however, only seem to heighten the sense of destiny. John Powell writes, "For the word *crisis*, the Chinese use a combination of two characters. These two characters are those which designate 'danger' and 'opportunity.'"[1]

I clearly remember the first funeral I ever attended. I was just fourteen, and the service was for a young man in our church my age who was killed in a gun accident. I was horrified and fascinated at the same time. How was it possible to be so alive one moment, full of hopes and dreams, only to be dead the next? Could it happen to me? I certainly didn't want to die—I desperately wanted to live to the fullest, but Lester hadn't wanted to die either. I was very much in love with life, with its possibilities and my place in it. Death was terrifying to me.

We can learn much from this passage of life about passion for

God. The potential of life is enhanced by the awareness of death. And so it is spiritually as well. What an amazing gift God gives each of us—the potential to live out our callings and purpose to the fullest, aware of the amazing life He has for us, aware of the emptiness of life without Him. The end of a life without Him is tragic.

The early season of our developing spiritual life is an exciting time, a wondering of purpose and a keen awareness that there is a life-and-death battle for the soul. When our love for God is new and fresh, it seems easy and natural to pray. I am often amazed as I hear young Christians tell of their miraculous answers to prayer—whether it's praying for a parking place, a job, or a critical need. Answers to our prayers, however, aren't always that immediate, and our hearts get distracted, pulled away. We "mature." In other words, we lose the vibrancy of our first love. How do we keep our passion for God?

## ~ *1* ~

## WHAT PASSION
## CAPTURES MY HEART?

*What doth the Lord require of thee? To love Him with all thy heart and all thy soul.*

DEUTERONOMY 10:12 KJV

*There are two reasons for loving God: No one is more worthy of our love, and no one can return more in response to our love. God deserves our love because He first loved us. His love for us was genuine because He sought nothing for Himself. . . . While we should not have ulterior motives for loving God, rewards will come. . . . Love is spontaneous. The only reward love seeks is someone to love. If you are looking for something else, it isn't love. . . . The soul that loves God expects nothing in return. If it did, then it would love that prize instead of God.*[2]

BERNARD OF CLAIRVAUX

When I think of this stage of our prayer lives—the stage of passion, idealism, and dreams—I see it as a wonderful passage. A roller coaster, yes. But I find that revisiting this stage keeps my faith and prayer life vital. My friend Clare used to sing a lovely song years ago that I have never forgotten, and I sing it to myself now and then: "May I never lose the wonder, ever precious, ever new./Then my heart will never wander from His love so kind and true."[3]

It is passion for Him that captures our hearts. But do we choose our loves, or do they just happen to us, a coincidence of geography, chemistry, and need? Current thought encourages us to "follow our bliss," claiming that the heart should determine our direction in life. But matters of the heart can be messy, like trying to pull apart cotton candy: "What *is* the essence of this thing? I only know it is sweet, and I want more."

Jesus says that where my *treasure* is, there will my heart be. Treasure is what I consider to be of utmost value. And sometimes it takes awhile to recognize true treasure because some treasures must be mined through diligent search. "Following my heart" can be suspiciously like "following my needs." Oswald Chambers wrote, "No love of the natural heart is safe unless the human heart has been satisfied by God first."[4] And the temptations of the world are not just for the young. I have found myself loving the *work* of God more than loving God—loving approval more than loving *Him*.

Augustine wrote in the midst of his tumultuous passions, trying to decide whether or not he should follow Christ (he knew it would mean giving up a woman): "Save me, O God, but not yet." And when finally his heart was fully captured by God, he prayed with insight: "Our hearts were made for Thee, O God, and are restless until they rest in Thee."[5] No one thing, no person—no matter how noble, how brightly packaged—is worthy of being king of our hearts, other than Jesus. All else will fail us.

Solomon wrote, "Keep your heart with all diligence, for out of it spring the issues of life" (Prov. 4:23 NKJV). How astounding, then, to read of the end of Solomon's life, this wise man with great achievements, whose pagan wives turned his heart away from following God

(1 Kings 11:1-6). It is essential to keep our hearts burning brightly with love for Him, because our hearts will love *something*. Our hearts are not trustworthy without being captured by Him. As Jeremiah wrote, "The heart is deceitful above all things and beyond cure. Who can understand it? I the LORD search the heart" (Jer. 17:9, 10).

Jesus was asked what the sign of His coming would be. He said, "As it was in the days of Noah, so it will be at the coming of the Son of Man" (Matt. 24:37). Noah's day was a time when the earth was filled with corruption and violence, a time like today, when the love of many grows cold. As I see the signs about me, I'm reminded to hold this life loosely. The time is short. Jesus warned, "Remember Lot's wife" (Luke 17:32). She was the woman who made her home in Sodom and was reluctant to leave it. In looking back, she lost her life (Gen. 19). Her home was her treasure, but it could not withstand the fire.

If ever there was a time to pray passionate prayers, it is now. It is a time to reexamine what is closest to our hearts. He asks us, "Do you love Me? Don't be afraid of the world. I have overcome it." We must let our fears go and allow Him to love us. He is a gracious God, and His ways are good. We can trust Him with our hearts. Paul encouraged the younger Timothy: "Fan into flames the spiritual gift God gave you when I laid my hands on you. For God has not given us a spirit of fear and timidity, but of power, love, and self-discipline" (2 Tim. 1:7 NLT).

*Prayer*
*Lord, do I know Your love so intimately*
*that my fears are leaving?*

In the dark days of the Reformation in Europe, Martin Luther wrote to a friend:

I am against those worrying cares which are taking the heart out of you. Why make God a liar in not believing his wonderful promises, when he commands us to be of good cheer, and to cast all our care upon him, for he will sustain us? Do you think he throws such words to the winds? What more can the devil do than slay us? Christ has died for sin once for all, but for righteousness he will not die but live and reign. Why then worry, seeing he is at the helm? He who has been our Father will also be the Father of our children."[6]

MARTIN LUTHER

O Lord Jesus Christ, it was not to plague us men but to save us that Thou didst say, "No man can serve two masters"—oh, that we might be willing to accept it by doing it, that is, by following Thee! Thou didst leave behind Thee the trace of Thy footsteps, Thou the holy pattern of the human race and of each individual in it, so that, saved by Thy redemption, they might every instant have confidence and boldness to follow Thee.[7]

KIERKEGAARD

~ *2* ~

## WHY MUST WE PRAY
## WITH PASSION?

*I have written to you, young men, because you are strong, and
the word of God abides in you, and you have overcome the
wicked one.*

1 JOHN 2:14 NKJV

Why must we pray with passion? Because lives are at stake. There is a
battle going on for our hearts and minds, not to mention the hearts
and minds of our children. As someone once said, "Our prayers must
mean something to us if they are to mean something to God."
Unrighteousness seems to prevail today, yet the Bible reminds us that
where "sin abounded, grace abounded much more" (Rom. 5:20
NKJV). Peter Taylor Forsyth, a pastor in the early part of the century,
put it well: "You must live with people to know their problems, and
live with God in order to solve them."[8]

Just last week our daughter Amy came home from a basketball
road trip deeply troubled. On the two-hour bus ride home, the girl sitting next to Amy told her she wanted to commit suicide. Caring people are trying to help the young woman, but her situation seems
desperate.

Amy was distressed over the girl's plight, and she began to tell me
how difficult it was for her in school, too—the profanity and the peer
pressure to do things that are not right. Amy's life has been a major

struggle compounded by some puzzling and paralyzing learning disabilities. School is one enormous set of mental and emotional hurdles for her every day. A few weeks ago, we were all in despair and were contemplating several other education options, but nothing seemed right.

The worst problem we faced was Amy's negative attitude toward herself. It is difficult to convince her of her worth when she is getting so many messages that she's a failure. Bill and I had been praying desperately for some kind of answer for Amy—but I never dreamed how God would answer those prayers! I wrote in my prayer journal some months ago, "Lord, I ask for Your intervention, Your divine provision for Amy. We need a miracle! It's the Red Sea deal, God—it doesn't look good behind us or in front. But like the persistent, nagging mother that I am, I plead for Your answer—because Your answer will be good!"

I told her that night, "Amy, God has a wonderful plan for your life, but Satan also has a plan for your life that is destructive. You must choose which plan to follow." I must say here that Bill and I feel that one of our most important callings is to pray for our children—to pray that their hearts and minds will be captured by the love of Jesus, because there are so many other competing "loves." The battle is for our hearts, and how keenly we feel it in youth, although the battle goes on throughout life.

That night we went to church, and I could sense that something was going on with Amy and God. For one thing, it was her idea to go to church (thirty miles away from home) even though we had to go straight from basketball practice and didn't have time even to have dinner. She sat next to me in the Wednesday night service, and tears rolled down her face as we sang worship songs. Amy is usually very shy and quiet, horrified at the thought of drawing attention to herself. But at the end of the service when the invitation was given for those to come forward who needed to commit their lives to Jesus Christ, she made a beeline for the altar with me in tow. It was a genuine conversion experience—Holy Spirit conviction, repentance, and a complete change. On the way home she said over and over, "I feel so clean. I feel light as a feather!"

She *is* changed. The very next day at school, Amy joined Campus Life (she was always too busy or too shy to go before), and she reads her Bible every day on her own, obviously hungry to grow. It is amazing to see up close how God rebuilds a life from the inside out when we turn to Him with our whole selves. Amy's heart has been captured by God, and it is beautiful to watch. Yes, she was raised in a Christian home with "Jesus for breakfast," so to speak, but it was her heart that needed Him, and so now He's there!

*Prayer changes things.* I remember being shattered by a relationship when I was in college, and maybe for the first time ever I was desperate for God. I was far from home; I was truly on my own and had tasted real disappointment for the first time. I found an altar and prayed . . . and prayed . . . and prayed. My words were incoherent; my tears and desperation said it all: "God, I throw myself wholly on You. Take me as I am. If you can, use me." I knew my parents were praying for me—and God answered their prayers. I'm reminded of the "hound of heaven" that pursues us through the prayers of God's people:

> *I fled Him down the nights and down the days.*
> *I fled Him down the arches of the years.*
> *I fled Him down the labyrinthine ways of my own mind*
> *And in the midst of tears I hid from Him,*
> *And under running laughter.*[9]

FRANCIS THOMPSON

*Prayer*
*Lord, am I cooperating with*
*Your plan for my life?*

*Multitudes, multitudes in the valley of decision! For the day of the Lord is near in the valley of decision.*

JOEL 3:14 NKJV

~ *3* ~

## WHO IS TEACHING
## ME TO PRAY?

*One of his disciples said to him, "Lord, teach us to pray, just as
John taught his disciples."*

LUKE 11:1

Rarely will someone offer to be your prayer mentor; most often you must look for one. I learned about prayer firsthand by watching my parents, as well as my husband's parents, who still pray faithfully and diligently for all of their family members. Years ago Grandma Ferlen, an older woman in our church, became a wonderful, rare mentor to me. She was a dynamic prayer warrior in the disguise of a four-foot-nine-inch "little old lady," with bright blue eyes. Every day she sat in her rocker and prayed for at least four hours for long lists of people in our community. My life wasn't like hers—I had three tiny children—but I learned from watching her life that prayer is a powerful dynamic available to all God's children. Her prayer life still impacts me today.

You may find your prayer mentor in an unlikely place. Study him or her. Take notes. Hang around and ask questions. Take someone to lunch whom you suspect has an active, vital prayer life and "pick his brain." Read and learn from the saints of old. Attend a prayer seminar, if possible, and ask others, "How do you pray?" Adapt these ideas to your own life. You can't be who they are, but you can learn from them.

Put on your antennas. Know what you *don't* want to be like. It takes discernment to find the right mentor. There are negative mentors out there, too, even in Christian circles who are not godly or healthy models. You must discern which role models are worth emulating and seek out experiences and opportunities that will stretch you in positive ways. It helps to know when and how and where others pray. One woman told me she could not survive without her "power shower"—as she did her most intense intercessory prayer and praise while she was in the shower.

In a survey I took of several hundred women in California, a majority of them said they prayed as they drove. (I would, too, if I drove California freeways!) But the idea is that we can pray anytime, anywhere, from our individual lives. The important thing is to learn from others and then simply decide to pray, learning as you go.

*Prayer*
*Lord, teach me to pray, both from godly*
*mentors and from Your example!*

Did you ever say anything like this to yourself, "It is so difficult to select a place"? What about the time when you were in love; was it impossible to select a place to meet in? No, it was far from impossible. . . .Think how long our Lord has waited for you; you have seen Him in your visions; now pray to Him. Get a place, not a mood, but a definite material place and resort to it constantly, and pray to God as His Spirit in you will help you.[10]

OSWALD CHAMBERS

As we grow in God, our prayer life will grow, too. To have a truly meaningful conversation with someone, you need to get to know that person. There are levels of relationship. On the surface level one carries on a casual conversation—such as saying, "Good morning," to someone on an elevator. Then there is another level where you exchange names and basic information. If you progress further in the relationship, you reach the level at which you share thoughts and feelings. You begin to trust each other with your hearts, with what is important to you. Over time, if the relationship progresses, you become involved in each other's lives as you invest time and interest in that person. A good relationship requires more than talking or sharing of one's self. It takes listening, response.

Growing in prayer is like this. Many of my beginning prayers were like those of the boy I mentioned in the Introduction, who was bagging my groceries—*I need help!* And as I've learned through Scripture, that's okay, especially for us rookies. God is open to the cry of His children.

But the more I walk with Him, the more I believe He longs for our fellowship, for prayer to be a two-way street. Jesus said, "Why do you call me, 'Lord, Lord,' and do not do what I say?" (Luke 6:46). There's a time when prayer leads to action, to obedience. Growing in prayer is a process. Prayer not only offers me the place to pour out my heart before Him, but prayer also provides a place to listen and to learn God's heart, to see the world as He does. Andrew Murray writes:

> In waiting upon God, the first thought is of *the God upon whom we wait.* We enter His presence and feel we need just to be quiet, so that He, as God, can overshadow us with Himself. Just be still before Him, and allow His Holy Spirit to waken and stir up in your soul the childlike disposition of absolute

dependence and confident expectation. Wait upon God as a Living Being, as the Living God, who notices you and is just longing to fill you with His salvation. Wait on God till you know you have met Him; prayer will then become so different.[11]

We can learn, too, by seeing how Jesus prayed, as well as by reading other prayers. Although the following prayers are simple—one-liners—they are some of the most powerful prayers ever prayed:

The lepers cried to Jesus, "Lord, Son of David, have mercy on us!" (Matt. 20:31 NLT). And Jesus did, and healed them.

David prayed after his sin with Bathsheba, "Create in me a clean heart, O God, and renew a steadfast spirit within me" (Ps. 51:10 NKJV). God restored and redeemed David.

The thief on the cross prayed, "Lord, remember me when You come into Your kingdom" (Luke 23:42 NKJV). And Jesus told him that he would be with Him that very day in Paradise.

Jesus prayed from the cross, "Father, forgive them, for they do not know what they do" (Luke 23:34 NKJV). This is a prayer that still astounds and moves us.

Jesus prayed for His disciples, "I pray for them. . . . I do not pray that You should take them out of the world, but that You should keep them from the evil one. . . . Sanctify them by Your truth. Your word is truth" (John 17:9, 15, 17 NKJV).

These prayers are powerful because they involve matters of life and death, forgiveness and repentance. They are *passionate* prayers.

*Prayer*
*Lord, may I learn from Your example*
*and from godly mentors to pray passionate prayers!*

Great talent is a gift of God, but it is a gift which is by no means necessary in order to pray well. This gift is required in order to converse well with men; but it is not necessary in order to speak well with God. For that, one needs good desires, and nothing more.[12]

ST. JOHN OF THE CROSS

~ *4* ~

## How Can I Pray for God's Purpose for Me?

*Remember your Creator in the days of your youth, before the days of trouble come.*

ECCLESIASTES 12:1

How can we pray for God's purpose for our lives? As a teenager at missionary services in our local church, I would sing with the congregation, "I'll go where you want me to go, dear Lord/O'er mountain, o'er plain, o'er sea./I'll be what you want me to be, dear Lord." Years later, when I was married and a young mother, I stood with Bill at his ordination service. Shivers went down my spine as we heard the awesome commission: *Preach the Word!* I accepted the challenge along with Bill and believed I had a purpose as well to share God's Word.

Now with life changing at a dizzying rate, I pray, "Lord, refresh my passion to live wholeheartedly for You!" There is no greater purpose than simply to be aware of the need to share what we have received. Our world is hungry for the priceless treasure, Jesus, and how important it is simply to be aware of those who need Him and to see our world as Jesus did, with eyes of compassion.

It seems that Jesus always shines the brightest from me when I allow people directly into my life. Despite my flaws and humanity, I want to give out of the abundance of what He has given me. I think back to a family in our neighborhood that came to Christ through our family, to an exchange student who asked me to teach her how to pray after she watched me pray for a sick friend, of a friend of our son who came to faith in Christ in our home.

What a simple yet profound gift it is just to pray for someone. Bill and Barbara New, dear friends of ours, have committed to pray for anyone God sends their way on Monday evenings in their home near Dallas, Texas. It is not unusual for nearly one hundred people to show up for an evening of prayer. How simple, yet how profound and powerful is prayer. It is the least we can do and the most we can do.

Pray that the Lord will show you needs in which you can best fulfill your purpose, and prayerfully consider how God can use you there. He does want to use you, and sometimes it takes awhile to find out exactly how and where. I have found that it's a lifetime journey of learning, of studying, of growing with God—a process of understanding your weaknesses as well as your strengths. Henry Blackaby wrote, "When God lets you know what He wants to do through you, it will be something only God can do. What you believe about Him will determine what you do. If you have faith in the God who called you, you will obey Him; and He will bring to pass what He has purposed to do. If you lack faith, you will not do what He wants. That is disobedience."[13]

This is something I am only now appreciating. I used to think that to speak or to write books I needed to generate knowledge from other places and use that material to speak to others. But I've learned that the only real material I have to deal with is me. And when I spend time in God's Word, in prayer, in honest journaling, and in honest dialog with others, I see that my prayer life can grow.

Our vulnerability at this place of purity of passion—and it is a wonderful place, make no mistake—is to run ahead and not listen, thinking prayer will always be like this. Answers will always be forthcoming. But prayer is more listening than talking. It's opening ourselves up to Him, learning to wait and wanting to grow. Our prayer lives will change as we grow, because to grow is to change.

*Prayer*
*Lord, am I praying wholeheartedly*
*for Your will for my life?*

~ *5* ~

## How Can My Prayer
## Life Grow?

*For the kingdom of heaven is like a man traveling to a far coun-*
*try, who called his own servants and delivered his goods to them.*
*And to one he gave five talents, to another two, and to another*
*one, to each according to his own ability. . . . For to everyone who*
*has, more will be given, and he will have abundance; but from*
*him who does not have, even what he has will be taken away.*

MATTHEW 25:14-15, 29 NKJV

*There are four ways in which He reveals His will to us—*
*through the Scriptures, through providential circumstances,*
*through the convictions of our own higher judgment, and*
*through the inward impressions of the Holy Spirit on our*
*minds.*

*The Scriptures come first. If you are in doubt upon any sub-*
*ject, you must first of all consult the Bible about it, and see*
*whether there is any law there to direct you. Until you have*
*found and obeyed God's will as it is there revealed, you must not*
*ask nor expect a separate direct personal revelation.*[14]

HANNAH WHITALL SMITH

It's one thing to have a vision of how you can grow, but it's possible, too,
to feel intimidated by the prayer style of another believer, wishing you
could pray with the same eloquence and authority. God values our individual personalities and gifts, and He wants to hear from us just as we are.
I've found it freeing to realize that there is no single "right" way to pray.

I have a friend with a dynamic prayer ministry. She is bold and assertive in her prayers, and I feel like a spiritual wimp in comparison. Another friend's ministry is not public, but her thoughtful and insightful prayers are focused and diligent. Both of these women are being used mightily by God.

Prayer is intensely private, and yet at times we are called upon to be public with it. I confess I'm more comfortable praying while I'm outside walking or while writing prayers in my journal early in the morning with my Bible and coffee before the family is up. It's easy for me to put my arms around my children and husband and pray with them.

I'm being stretched though. I serve as a member of the prayer team of our church, which means I make myself available after the services to pray with people who desire prayer. I am learning that it's important to prepare my own heart for prayer ministry by first silently asking God to purify my heart, to give me a listening ear to His Holy Spirit. How important it is to pray with humility and trust, knowing I am simply God's servant. He is doing the work; I don't have to "generate" the answer, and I'm grateful that God uses us in our individual personalities and gifts.

A young woman told me that she is in a Bible study with several other young women who are not used to praying in front of others. But they are all growing in this area, helped along by a sense of humor and thoughtfulness. Here's the bottom line: It's dangerous to compare your spirituality with another person's. God looks on the heart. He wants to use us as we are, where we are.

I enjoy a different type of communication with each of my children, as they are all different. And so we, God's children, are different from each other. Yes, there are common threads—it is our heart that God longs for, that He seeks out. Perhaps blending our prayers and praises together, we are a unique fragrance to Him, a beautiful bouquet of praise and honor.

*Prayer*
*Lord, may I have faith to believe I can grow deeper*
*in my prayers and bear more fruit because of it!*

*Continue earnestly in prayer,*
*being vigilant in it with thanksgiving.*

COLOSSIANS 4:2 NKJV

It is amazing that a poor human creature is able to speak with God's high majesty in heaven and not be afraid. When we pray, the heart and the conscience must not pull away from God because of our sins and our unworthiness, or stand in doubt, or be scared away. When we pray, we must hold fast and believe that God has heard our prayer. It was for this reason that the ancients defined prayer as an *Ascensus mentis ad Deum*, "a climbing up of the heart unto God."[15]

MARTIN LUTHER

SIGNS YOUR PRAYER LIFE IS GROWING

*Listen, listen to me, and eat what is good, and your soul will delight in the richest of fare. Give ear and come to me; hear me, that your soul may live.*

ISAIAH 55:2-3

Sooner or later we need to grow up! As they say, "Growing old is mandatory; growing up is optional." Here are four signs that your prayer life is growing:

*Your prayers deal with more than yourself.*

Everything's not all about you! You pray for others' needs, others' pain. Your prayers sound less like grocery lists, and you say more often, "Lord, what is Your will in this matter?" and you say, "Yes, Lord," to some pretty wild things.

Moses was called to lead the children of Israel out of Egypt (they'd been there over 400 years—almost twice as long as the United States has been a nation!). A tough, tough calling to deliver people who didn't actually want to be delivered. As difficult as their lives were, the Israelites were very entrenched in Egypt. Canaan was but a dim memory. Nevertheless, Moses received clear direction from God, even though at first he was reluctant to obey.

As you grow up spiritually, you begin to have an understanding of the Big Picture, and you can pray bigger prayers. You begin to see that the Big Picture transcends personality. The journey back to Canaan was a project greater than Moses. He died on this side of the Jordan and didn't get to cross over into the Promised Land, as great a leader as he was. But Joshua stepped up to the plate, got direction from God, and went on, not threatened by Moses' previous success nor his mistakes.

*You begin to pray about what your life message is saying.*

If your life is to nourish others, you must ask: "What lies within me that others want?" It begins with an awareness that your life is a gift—a unique, precious gift—and if Jesus, God's Son, needed to come away frequently to quiet places to talk to His Father, how much more do we need it? Without coming away, we do not feed ourselves, we do not develop our life message. It takes time. Study. Listening.

When Joshua and the leaders finally crossed over the Jordan, part of their instruction was to take "provisions for themselves" (Josh. 1:11). We must learn to "feed" ourselves in order to develop a life message. How absolutely essential it is in our noisy lives to take the time to think, to reflect on what our life message is, and then to take the responsibility to see that we are nourished spiritually. We can blame those around us or whine that we're not "getting fed," but a sign of growing up is taking the responsibility to nourish our spiritual lives by Bible study and prayer.

> Before you can truly pray, let alone achieve any more refined feats of spirituality or service, you have first of all got to make sure that you are really there. And the discipline of simply staying in your [prayer] cell is intended to bring you face to face with yourself and with your real needs and capacities. . . . Without this foundation of self-knowledge and realism, any attempt to help other people will founder.[16]
>
> SIMON TUGWELL

*You grow to see problems as opportunities to pray.*

I love the worship chorus, "You are awesome in this place, mighty God./You are awesome in this place, Abba Father!" When I sing about "this place," I am reminded of the places where I am most uncomfortable, most lonely, most at the end of myself—places I know well. But "this place" is also where I have the opportunity to see our awesome God.

Jacob was running away because he was in trouble with his family. In a lonely place far from home, he experienced the presence of God out under the stars. He said, "Surely the Lord is in this place, and I did not know it. . . . How awesome is this place!" (Gen. 28:16-17 NKJV)

I told you about Grandma Ferlen, an elderly lady whose prayer life dramatically impacted mine. I would sit at her feet with my small babies and often be moved to tears in her presence, because it was as if we were carrying on a three-way conversation—me, Grandma Ferlen, and God. She prayed amazing prayers of faith. On her list though was her son who did not know God. When Grandma Ferlen died at age ninety-two, she left me her Bible. Her favorite passage that she quoted often was "I know whom I have believed and am persuaded that He is able to keep what I have committed to Him until that day" (2 Tim. 1:12 NKJV). Why, I wondered, did God answer so many of her prayers of faith and yet not the one closest to her heart?

Only now do I understand her clinging to this verse, her clinging to the one to whom she committed her dearest burden. Just this year

I heard that her son recently came to faith in Christ at age sixty-six—years after his mother's death. Grandma Ferlen prayed with confidence because in her life of prayer, she grew to know Him, and in knowing Him, she learned to trust Him.

Her life of prayer is like a beacon to me, reminding me to persist in this holy pursuit, knowing prayers are not wasted, not futile, even if our prayers concern impossible problems. Our prayers are a precious fragrance in God's sight and present us with the opportunity to come to the one to whom we can commit everything, knowing He is able, knowing we can trust Him.

*You grow to recognize His voice.*

> *The sheep listen to his voice. He calls his own sheep by name and leads them out. When he has brought out all his own, he goes on ahead of them, and his sheep follow him because they know his voice.*

> JOHN 10:3-4

A few years ago when we had our two springer spaniels, Norman and Walter, I took them to the meadow where they could run freely. I'm sorry to say they were not very obedient dogs (which probably has more to do with their owner than anything). But it was a gorgeous spring day, and the earth had a musky, warm smell to it, and red-winged blackbirds, like exotic ornaments, bobbed on the limbs of willow trees. A chipmunk darted across our path, and Walter bolted, nearly pulling me over. "Hey, wait until we get to the meadow!" I knew if I let them off the leashes while we were still in the neighborhood, there would be trouble, especially with Norman, who was prone to wander. Oh, he eventually came back, but he always took the long way and often was deaf to my calls. Then he would return, innocent, smiling, asking how I was.

We reached the meadow and crawled under the barbed wire fence, and I let the dogs go. Off they bounded, ears flopping as they jumped over logs, following their noses, going crazy with all the tantalizing scents. I followed them to the edge of the meadow, sat down on the grass, and leaned against a tree, basking in the sun and the quiet beauty of the scene, glad for this moment of peace.

I heard in the distance a voice calling, and I looked up to see a woman standing on the other side of the meadow, walking her dog. As she called to her dog, Norman and Walter ran toward her. Exasperated, I stood and yelled at them, calling them back. Finally they wheeled around, realizing where I was. They came back to me and dropped by my side panting. "You silly things," I scolded. "Don't you know my voice?"

*"Do you know My voice?"*

It was one of those moments when I knew God was talking to me. I sat quietly, waiting. Outwardly it would seem that not much had changed with me in the last few years—same husband, family, all growing older through the natural progressions of life. And yet I had an inner hunger that cried, "Lord, I'm not satisfied with the status quo! I want to take the next step, to experience You fully in my life, to live for You as never before." I don't want to just cope, to make it through life to heaven, safe at last. Growth is much easier to measure when I look at visible things—opportunities, success, innovative ministry. Tangible things. And yet our Lord says, "Take My yoke upon you and learn of Me." And sitting at My feet—getting to know Me—this is "the good part, which will not be taken away" (Luke 10:42 NKJV).

I've noticed that on my walks in the winter when the snow is deep, the dogs stay close to me. But in springtime—watch out! And that's true with me, too. During the hard, stormy times of my life, I hold close to my Good Shepherd's hand. But when the sunny meadow of life is sweet, and I have an illusion of my own strength, *that is when I must know His voice as never before.* I realize that I must know Him as my Source, not just a *resource.* I must grow in the fruit of the Spirit, in my home and in my most intimate relationships, where I'm known best.[17]

It seems to me that staying where God has us, being true to our callings and commitments, is where we grow. It is within that crucible, knowing how to be there by studying the Word, as George Mueller said, "on my knees," that we grow to recognize His voice and respond to Him, being quick to obey.

### Prayer of Praise

*Lord, I praise You for ideals and dreams that stir passion in me to live for You with all my heart. May I have a renewed sense of knowing the joy of finding my purpose and calling in You.*

*Teach me the disciplines necessary to grow into a prayer warrior who grapples with the outcome of spiritual kingdoms. May I learn to pray with consistency and constancy.*

*And may I continually praise You for Your mighty works.*
*In Jesus' name, amen.*

The most neglected piece of real estate in the world is the ground whereon you stand. It may seem unpromising; it may not be the site that you would choose. But there was Moses in the desert. He had had every advantage in the Egyptian court. For a time he had seemed to be gaining leadership among his own people, whom he sought to free. And he settled down in midlife, a failure.

But the voice came across the shimmering sand amidst the burning sagebrush. *The ground whereon you stand is holy ground!* And from that place Moses went forth to save a people and to found a kingdom. The most neglected piece of real estate in the world is the ground whereon you stand.[18]

HARRY EMERSON FOSDICK

*Prayer*
*Lord, do You have more of me now than You did ten years ago?*
*Do I know Your voice so intimately that I am quick to respond?*

WAYS TO GROW: REKINDLING THE PASSION

> *Oh come, let us worship and bow down;*
> *Let us kneel before the Lord our Maker.*
> *For He is our God, and we are the people of His pasture,*
> *and the sheep of His hand.*
> *Today, if you will hear His voice: Do not harden your hearts.*

PSALM 95:6-8 NKJV

᠕ Think about what is closest to your heart. In your prayer journal write a prayer to God, offering that place to Him. Ask: What hinders me from loving God with all my heart? Perhaps it's busy-ness, selfishness, unbelief. Spend some time in worship (try Ps. 103) and ask for an undivided heart toward God.

᠕ God asks us to come with faith, into His Presence with praise. (In your prayer time, *consciously* come into His presence with praise and thanksgiving.) Does this dynamic affect how you hear His voice?

᠕ What is your greatest difficulty, your most persistent struggle right now? Present this to our Lord and ask Him to speak to you here. He says, "Come away, My beloved." It is in the secret places, in knowing His Word, worshiping Him, that we are restored, that He speaks to us.

᠕ Think about a "place"—perhaps a room or a chair—where you keep your Bible and your prayer journal, where you meet God. Perhaps it is outside as you take a "prayer walk" or a "praise walk." *Cultivate, protect that place.*

᠕ Remember what it was like when you first knew the Lord—perhaps you are in that place now, or perhaps you are not there yet. Spend time with Him as you did at first—worshiping Him, asking for His direction in your life.

*Prayer Exercises*

There are as many different ways to pray as there are different kinds of people and situations. Be flexible and creative with your "idea" of prayer and grow to consider other ways of praying. Write a prayer of:

- Adoration

- Thanksgiving

- Confession

- Intercession

One life yielded to God at all costs is worth thousands only touched by God.

OSWALD CHAMBERS

Men must worship something; if they do not worship an unseen Being who loves and cares for them, they will worship the works of their own hands; they will secretly bow down to the things that they see, and hear, and taste, and smell; these will be their lords and master.[19]

FREDERICK DENISON MAURICE

*Reflections*

*Reflections*

# MIDLIFE

## DESPERATION FOR GOD
## IN HARD TIMES

∽🕾

*Lord, You know my heart and my deepest agonies, my conflicts. I long to live a focused life of purpose, of love and goodness. But life trips me up, Lord. I get ambushed by my own humanity and by others' humanity. I don't understand why certain things happen. At times life does not seem fair.*

*Often I am plunged into a deep sense of failure, and, yes, terror grips me as the losses and disappointments of life at times are overwhelming. Father God, my life is irretrievably broken without Your touch. However, You are greater than my failure, and I ask You to forgive my debts as I forgive my debtors. Please deliver me from the evil one.*

*Lord, I ask for Your divine intervention, because "whom have I on earth beside Thee?" I am desperate without You. Amen.*

∽🕾

O God, listen to my cry! Hear my prayer!
From the ends of the earth, I will cry to you for help,
    for my heart is overwhelmed.
Lead me to the towering rock of safety,
    for you are my safe refuge.

PSALM 61:1-2 NLT

*Three*

# UNSOLVED
# MYSTERIES

⤧

*God, my God, I yelled for help, and you put me together.*
*God, you pulled me out of the grave, gave me another*
*chance at life when I was down and out.*

PSALM 30:2
(THE MESSAGE)

⤧

The third painting of Thomas Cole's *Journey of Life* shows a man
with a terrified expression on his face, sailing down a stormy river
in what looks like whitewater. There are huge boulders in the
rapids, and danger is evident. The painting depicts the unpre-
dictability, the potential for disaster that often presents itself in
midlife. Our twenty-something sons love to go whitewater rafting
on the Deschutes River near where we live. Bill has gone, too, but I
don't like it. Give me still waters any day—in life as well as on the
water. Many of us know more about this place of "whitewater" than
we would like—times when expectations and reality clash, times
of illness and major loss. Often this stormy passage poses many
questions and few answers. I knew I was in trouble when I saw that

this section of the book was twice as long as the others, and I have had to drastically cut for space.

There are some mysteries about which we must pray, "God, why is this happening?" The stage of midlife with all its twists and turns is not just an actual physical state (which is where I am age-wise), but it's also a spiritual passage that can confront us any time. It can affect the very young as well.

The good news is that along with the danger, there is opportunity. The danger lies in giving in to the difficulties. One woman recently told me she has given up and is just going through the motions because it seems that God isn't hearing her prayers. Her husband of twenty years, a former Promise Keeper, is drinking heavily, and their relationship has deteriorated.

May I say with much gentleness—don't give up and don't be afraid of confronting your desperate needs through prayer! In a survey I did, over 100 individuals wrote honestly about their most desperate time ever. I was moved to tears as I read many of their stories of how they were turned inside out against life and how God met them in amazing ways. Jesus didn't say, "In the off-chance a storm will come," or in the "rare occurrence of a storm." He did say, "In the world you will have tribulation; but be of good cheer, I have overcome the world" (John 16:33 NKJV). Storms are an inevitable part of life, and they will come.

While this midlife place is hard—and nobody likes pain—it is also the richest place of life spiritually, because this is where we come face to face with God in the midst of our own desperate needs, if we seek Him. An unknown author wrote, "God's greatest gifts to us often are disguised—wrapped in problems, trials, and sufferings." This place is where He refines us and makes us people of real love and compassion. In this tumultuous time, how desperately we need to hear and know truth. Real truth. I am humbled by all I do not know. But one thing I do know about this place in life: It's a time to pray as never before. As we read through the gospel accounts of Jesus' life on earth, we see how He met people at their point of need—their blindness, sickness, and despair. And He will meet us, too, when we pray.

> The poet has expression, the sage meditates, the righteous man acts; but he who is on the frontier of the divine world prays, and his prayer is expression, meditation, and action all in one.... The universe belongs to him who will, who can, who knows how to pray.[1]
>
> ROWLAND P. QUILTER

~ *1* ~

## TIME TO PRAY TO
## KNOW THE TRUTH

*Cleanse me from secret faults.*
*Keep back Your servant also from presumptuous sins;*
*Let them not have dominion over me. . . .*
*Let the words of my mouth and the meditation of my heart be*
*acceptable in Your sight, O Lord, my strength and my Redeemer.*

PSALM 19:12-14 NKJV

*At every plateau of despondency, Christ came—I knew He loved*
*me, yet I fled. I did not want His presence, for it reminded me of*
*my unfulfilled desire to please Him.* [2]

CALVIN MILLER

There is a connection with being "real"—knowing the truth about who and where we are—and knowing God. When we approach our awesome God with brokenness and no defenses, He is there. The truth is, we are all desperate without Him, and the place of "whitewater" is a pointed reminder.

My friend Mattie Ann, who was diagnosed with advanced pancreatic cancer, told me: "It's God-time! Doctors have told me they've done everything possible for me. So now I am in His hands." The truth about ourselves can be dismal, devastating. The invincibility we sense in the stage of youth is gone. I tend to avoid the truth about hard, perplexing situations. I don't like them.

I think back to several summers ago when one of our sons was deeply disillusioned by a Christian leader on a missions trip, a situation still difficult for me to understand. Not long ago I listened to my daughter Amy pour out her tears over failing again on a test when she'd worked so hard. "Why doesn't my brain work like other people's?" she stormed. "Why did God let me have encephalitis when I was a baby? Why did my birth mother leave me?"

But I have seen that when we finally get to the place of realizing that the formulas don't work, then we see the truth of our own hearts and of our own desperation without Him. We see that He does work in His way and in His time. And His timing is always perfect, as He makes all things beautiful in His time. All that we commit to Him is safe—even our most desperate and painful needs. John Chrysostom said, "Find the door of your heart, and you will discover it is the door of the kingdom of God."[3]

## DISCERNING OUR TIMES

Ecclesiastes 8:5-6 says that "a wise woman's heart discerns both time and judgment, because for every matter there is a time and judgment." To effectively pray at this place in life, I believe it helps to discern—or understand—the times. The place of "whitewater" can be a time of reevaluation, of understanding that we are indeed finite, and we begin to have the courage to really look at our lives. It is a time perhaps of reaping from some of the habits we have sown, the lifestyles that we have chosen, the values that we have lived. It is just a place where life happens.

When we are confronted by the hard things of life, it's time to stop and pay attention, to be thoughtful and reflective to discern how we should pray. There are many at this place who rush past it, denying the obvious questions and issues. Here we may try to hold onto patterns of the past or be tempted to radically depart from our set course to reinvent ourselves or take matters into our own hands. But our prayers can start to become powerful as we learn to pray with discernment and wait for God to move in His way in the situation.

It helps to discern not only our personal times but also the times of the world around us that deeply affects us and all we hold dear—our children and grandchildren, our work and our callings. We must understand how to pray in these challenging times.

*What characterizes our time?*

- ॐ *It is a lawless time.* Respect for the rule of law that we assumed would always be in our land is no longer there. Instead, it is now as it was described in Judges 21:25 when "everyone did what was right in his own eyes." This belief subtly but deeply affects all of us.

- ॐ *It is a time of shifting values.* Right has become wrong; wrong has become right. Value is determined by marketability to the current cultural hunger. From education to the media, the values that dominate our culture influence everything.

- ॐ *It is an accelerated time.* Dr. Richard Hoffman of New York says that civilization's three major killers are not heart disease, cancer, and accidents, but calendars, telephones, and clocks. Why is it that we feel more pressure, behind the curve all the time? A recent study on Americans and their free time actually uncovered that Americans really do have more free time than they used to. They just don't feel like it because their sense of the necessary has increased. It isn't enough to have a computer; we must have E-mail and a web site. Our cell phones have become necessities. Many on my prayer surveys told how they did their praying "on the run." Their lives are hectic. We all have many meetings and organizations to attend, besides our family responsibilities.

⁓ *It is a spiritually hungry time.* "Spirituality" is "in"—yet it's a biblically ignorant time. We live in a land of many gods—a pagan land. We must know our God, know His Word, and as we allow Him to change us and be more and more at home in our lives, we can influence our world. Our times offer amazing opportunities for us, His followers.

⁓ *It is, more than ever, time to pray*—because the needs are desperate. Secular magazines are full of articles and interviews on prayer. There are current studies on prayer. People are fascinated; they're talking about prayer. Why? Because they know there is power in prayer. Prayer, however, is really just a symptom, an outgrowth, a consequence of a relationship with God.

Regardless of what's going on in our lives, we can pray from where we are. Anne told me, "I was having hard times in life, and it was difficult for me to pray. But a change happened after I discovered this pattern of praying: I first enter into praise; secondly, confession; third, thanksgiving; and then I present my needs to God. It has changed my life. I have a long way to go, but He's with me!"

*Prayer*
*Lord, open my eyes to the truth*
*of my life and of my need for You!*

O God my Father, I have no words, no words by which I dare express the things that stir within me. I lay bare myself, my world, before you in the quietness. Brood over my spirit with your great tenderness and understanding and judgment, so that I will find, in some strange new way, strength for my weakness, health for my illness, guidance for my journey. This is the stirring of my heart, O God, my Father. Amen.[4]

HOWARD THURMAN

~ *2* ~

## TIME TO FIND
## THE SECRET PLACE

*He who dwells in the secret place of the Most High shall abide
under the shadow of the Almighty.*

PSALM 91:1 NKJV

When I was a girl on the farm in Montana, I often had a secret place as
my refuge from a big and noisy family. Sometimes my secret place was
in the hayloft of the barn. Once it was in a grove of willow trees at the
end of a lane. If a granary was empty, it made a great secret place. I
could bolt the door from the inside, and no one could get in without
my permission. When my place got "found out" by my little brothers
or sisters, I had to find a new place. It must be my place, and mine
alone, to be quiet. In my secret place I would listen to the doves in the
rafters of the barn, or if I was outside, feel the wind on my face and see
the swallows wheeling against the sky. Often I would think about God
and talk to Him and dream about what I would be when I grew up.

As I grew older, I forgot about my secret place. I was busy, very
involved in church, in school activities, in music. I married, had children, and the secret place gradually became a distant childhood
memory.

In the summer following four long years of illness and a doctor's
ultimate diagnosis of "stress," I wondered what to do with the truth of
my life. That entire summer I memorized Psalm 91. I thought on it,

prayed it, wondered what it meant to dwell in the secret place with the Most High. It was all the Scripture reading and study I could manage that summer, but it awakened in me a homesickness for my secret place. "God," I prayed, "how do I find a secret place with You in my crammed-full life? How do I encounter You here? God, do You see the heavy burdens I carry? I need to talk to You alone. I am sick of myself, of trying to solve everything. Life is too complex for me, Father."

Just as in my childhood when I had to go look for the secret place, to make a conscious choice to find it, I found the "secret place" again. The actual, physical place where you meet God may have to change from time to time, depending on what's going on in your life. But essentially I have found that it is a place where I come alone, a place where I am honest with God. It is a place of worship, a place of waiting. Although there are times to agree in prayer with fellow believers, this secret place must be private. It may be outside; walking works for me. For others, it's while driving. Sometimes I can find a quiet room in the house.

I believe we all need places to be alone with God, especially in our most challenging times of life. And our hectic and invasive times require solitude more than ever, although it's always been true that we must come away. Nearly 600 years ago, Thomas à Kempis wrote, "He that seeketh to attain to the more inward and spiritual things of religion must with Jesus draw apart from the crowd. . . . In silence and in stillness a soul advantageth itself and learneth the mysteries of Holy Scripture. There it findeth rivers of tears wherein it may every night wash and cleanse itself, that it may be so much the more familiar with its Creator, by how much the farther off it liveth from all worldly disquiet."[5]

But the secret place is not just a physical place; it's a place in the spirit, a place where God says, "You feel inadequate? Good. Meet me here! I am El Shaddai." The secret place is different from time to time. But it has a similar theme—it is a place where I see my helplessness against life and throw myself on God's mercy.

Sometimes it is a place of contention, a place of wrestling with God during crises for myself, family members, or friends. These are times of intercessory prayer where it seems that the issues are plain. Righteousness versus unrighteousness. A place to "get ahold of God," as the old saints would say. Instant answers? Not always. Sometimes months, years of waiting pass, and then the answers are often unexpected, surprisingly wonderful beyond belief. Sometimes the answer is to wait.

The secret place has often been for me a place of disillusionment. How painful it can be to let go of idols. But in the secret place, none can stand before Him. God alone is God. The secret place is often a place of loss. Isaiah said, "In the year that King Uzziah died, I saw the Lord" (6:1). When I lose people, things, positions—all the lovely things that charm me most—I am left standing empty-handed and yet strangely comforted because then I see the Lord. And in Him is restoration, peace, and forgiveness.

The "secret place" is not a place just to visit, but it is a place to abide, to dwell. Coming there requires being aware of where I am most afraid, most confused, most worried—and then inviting God into those places. It is humbling to be weak, but that is how God becomes strong in us. The prophet Isaiah urges us, "Come, my people, enter your chambers, and shut your doors behind you; hide yourself, as it were, for a little moment" (Isa. 26:20 NKJV).

*Prayer*
*O God, may I never neglect*
*to seek You in the secret place!*

*God resists the proud, but gives grace to the humble. Therefore submit to God. Resist the devil and he will flee from you. Draw near to God and He will draw near to you.... Humble yourselves in the sight of the Lord, and He will lift you up.*

JAMES 4:6-7, 10 NKJV

O Lord my God, when the storm is loud, and the night is dark, and the soul is sad, and the heart oppressed; then as a weary traveler, may I look to you; and beholding the light of your love, may it bear me on, until I learn to sing your song in the night. Amen.[6]

GEORGE DAWSON

~ *3* ~

## TIME TO GET RID
## OF OLD "STUFF"

*Create in me a clean heart, O God; and renew a right*
*spirit within me.*

PSALM 51:10 KJV

*Detachment is often understood as letting loose of what is*
*attractive. But it can also mean being attached to your own hate.*
*As long as you look for retaliation, you are riveted to your own*
*past. . . . When you dare to let go and surrender one of those*
*many fears, your hand relaxes and your palms spread out in a*
*gesture of receiving.*[7]

HENRI NOUWEN

One sunny day not long ago I realized that our house was definitely showing the effects of two years of book deadlines and speaking, not to mention twenty years of bringing more stuff in than we took out. Oh, I managed to keep a semblance of order, but my house was fast approaching critical mass—the clutter now overflowing onto counters and things bulging out of drawers. It was time to stop and do some deep cleaning.

I knew this would be no simple task, so I went room by room, starting in the attic and doing a little each day—one drawer, one closet. I've been at it for two months now, and I still have the kitchen and our bedroom and bathroom yet to go. My cleaning project often gets derailed though, because as I clean out a drawer or closet, I find things to linger over, such as a romantic card from Bill or snapshots of friends and family. A letter from Chris shortly after he went away to college thanking me for teaching him "the important things" made me cry. I uncovered a report Andy did in high school in which he wrote, "Our big, old softhearted house has more memories than New York City has people." He went on to write about them, and I found myself laughing. I found some sports clippings from when Jon and Eric were in high school (what high hopes we all had for basketball!) and some pencil drawings by Amy. These things I put with my children's scrapbooks. This cleaning-out process has made me realize how I cherish our "big, old softhearted" house.

But there's a lot of junk, too, that needs to be discarded, besides things to give away. I am slowly making progress with my deep cleaning, and it feels good to have my house becoming more streamlined, more efficient. After all, the house cannot live up to its potential when it's choked by too much stuff.

## GOD DOES NOT FIT

As I cleaned, I thought, *This is so like me! I have a tendency to cling to things with a tenacious grip. Not just physical things, but people. Positions. Memories.* I heard someone once say, "The Lord will not fit in an occupied heart." I wonder—is my heart too crowded for Him, so full of my own agenda that there's no room for Him to tell me His?

How necessary it is to evaluate periodically what's filling my life and, as Hebrews says, to "strip off every weight that slows us down, especially the sin that so easily hinders our progress" (Hebrews 12:1 NLT). It's so easy to allow things into our lives. Like clutter, hurts and offenses can pile up, but if God gently but distinctly puts His finger on something in my life, how essential it is to obey and let go of it. "Old stuff" can begin to define and control my life if I do not yield.

I must want obedience to God more. I must want God's approval more and not draw back from the very real pain of letting go. The wonderful thing about obedience is that when we respond to God with a yes in these matters, we become closer to Him, more intimate, as obedience to Him brings a fresh understanding of His holiness.[8]

Various reasons can keep us from hearing what God is saying to us about what it means to get rid of the things that hinder us, that choke His life out of us. Ask yourself, "Is there a theme that grips my life?" Perhaps it's an injustice done to us—some great wrong. Injustices are difficult to bear, and we can become consumed by them.

## FORGIVENESS AND PRAYER

Jesus clearly said that failure to forgive blocks our prayers, and if necessary, we must forgive seventy times seven (Matt. 18:21-35). He also said, "If you are offering your gift at the altar and there remember that your brother has something against you, leave your gift there in front of the altar. First go and be reconciled to your brother; then come and offer your gift" (Matt. 5:23-24). We must deal with unforgiveness before it hardens into bitterness, because a root of bitterness has enormous destructive potential.

Not long ago a volunteer firefighter knocked at our door telling us what we needed to do in case of fire. Our local fire department here on the edge of the National Forest is vigilant, cautious. In the spring we must rake dried brush and pine needles from around the house. A few years ago after someone had burned dead brush and tree stumps, a fire began to smolder underground, going through the root system. Our soil, formed of lava thousands of years ago, in some places is so porous and rocky with air pockets that the fire was actually able to burn underground. The fire came above ground a few miles away, surprising everyone with its consuming intensity, and destroyed some of the forest and several homes—all from a fire in the root system below ground!

Roots are an efficient network, feeding the plant, making it grow. Some roots, especially young ones, come out easily when pulled. But then there are those stubborn ones that go deep. They are the ones that have a history, that have been allowed to flourish, that have been nurtured.

It reminds me of the root of bitterness. How does bitterness grow?

Bitterness comes from justice denied. A hope quenched. An expectation unmet. Anger grown cold and unresolved, maybe from an offense at the hands of people we love. How easily it happens and then takes root. We think, *He should have known better*, or, *If he would just say he is sorry*, or, *She needs to make restitution for this*, or, *God could have prevented this from happening, and He didn't*. I can be bitter at myself, too, mentally flogging myself for past mistakes. Or I can be bitter at the unrighteous in our nation, thinking in some twisted way I'm doing God a favor by being mad at sinners. Maybe it comes from wishing I were in God's place, thinking, *This wouldn't have happened if I were in charge.* Bitterness comes from a belief that I deserved better than I received. Bitterness is nasty stuff.

We've got to let go of it, or it destroys us. Walter Brueggeman writes, "We do not quickly divest ourselves. But the question will have been put. Can restlessness satisfy? Can greed secure? An invitation will have been issued. Return to the God who rests and gives rest, who sets free and satisfies.... Obedience is the daily task of yielding more regions of our life to God's sovereign purpose. We do not yield easily. But this tradition makes clear that if we do not yield, we shall die."[9]

And I find that the more life experience I have, the more opportunities I have for bitterness. The amazing thing is how it can color an entire life—how it can suddenly spring up, defiling and destroying everything in its path, and I wonder saying, "Where did that come from?" Injustices do happen. People can do terrible things to us. But forgiveness simply means releasing the offense into God's hands and letting Him be God. "Vengeance is Mine, I will repay," God says. As Walter Wangerin describes it: "Forgiveness is a sort of divine absurdity. It is irrational, as the world reasons things, and unwise. but 'has not God made foolish the wisdom of the world?' . . . For-give-ness is a holy, complete, unqualifed *giving.*"[10]

I receive healing from bitterness when I see my own desperate need for forgiveness. This awareness softens the hard ground that surrounds this stubborn root—even when I can't deal with the root itself. As I let go, He deals with it. "It is of the Lord's mercies," the prophet wrote in Lamentations 3:22, "that we are not consumed" (KJV).

Restoration is the work of grace. Hebrews 12: 28 urges, "Let us have grace." Verse 15 encourages us to keep "looking carefully lest anyone fall short of the grace of God; lest any root of bitterness springing up cause trouble, and by this many become defiled" (Heb. 12:15 NKJV).

Forgiveness is often not a one-time act. Some stubborn roots need more attention, just as some chronic wounds need more applications of ointment. I need His mercy new every morning, just like breakfast. Grace received again . . . and again . . . and again. And then I may freely offer it to others in need.

*Prayer*
*Lord, are there things I am stubbornly holding onto*
*that I must let go? Show me if I have caused bitterness*
*in someone else. I give it all to You.*

Two works of mercy set a man free: forgive and you will be forgiven, and give and you will receive.[11]

AUGUSTINE

~ *4* ~

# TIME TO PRAY
# WHAT YOU KNOW

*We are to be so deeply rooted in the love of Christ that we can stand up to any emotional earthquake, storm, or any form of discouragement. Knowing God as our Father also means to "grasp how wide and long and high and deep is the love of Christ, and to know this love that surpasses knowledge."*[12]

JAMES HOUSTON

Why does it seem at times that God doesn't answer prayer? Once my son was in a triple overtime basketball game at the state tournament, and I prayed most earnestly (with faith believing) that he would make his free throws so that the Redmond Panthers would win. I secretly hoped the mothers of the opposing team weren't praying. Maybe they were, because we lost! Or maybe the opponents were just a better team.

Okay, I realize basketball games are one thing, but life and death matters are another. When my father got cancer the year I turned twenty-nine, I prayed desperately that he would be healed. When he died, I questioned God. Why didn't He answer my prayers? Surely it is God's will that our families stay intact.

As I look back, I still don't know the answer. Nor do I understand why my brother-in-law and my sister-in-law lost a baby to SIDS. I only know that trust is a huge part of prayer, accepting that God's answers reflect His ultimate wisdom. Yes, I have seen God intervene in response to prayer. I personally have been physically and emotionally healed. I have witnessed miraculous answers to prayer for provision and protection in our family. And yet at other times God has remained silent despite my most desperate cries. As I look back through the years, I agree with author Jean Ingelow: "I have lived to thank God that all my prayers have not been answered."[13]

Years ago Bill and I were trying to buy a small house to use for a much-needed office. However, in the midst of our negotiations, the zoning was changed. We earnestly prayed, convinced we were supposed to have that building, which seemed perfect for our needs. Yet the harder we tried to complete the transaction, the more frustrated were our efforts. We finally gave up, full of questions. We had no idea then that a year later, a better building at a better price would become available. We could only look back later with a sigh of relief and say, "Thank You, Lord!"

Only God knows the future, and just because I don't receive an answer the way I think I should at the time doesn't mean God is ignoring my prayers. Sometimes God answers our prayers the way we answer our children: "No," "Not now," "Wait," or, "Yes!"

I used to think that to "pray in Jesus' name" literally meant to say, "in Jesus' name," and the deed would be done. Now I'm learning that to pray in Jesus' name means to pray according to His will. And it takes time to wait on Him, to study His Word to understand what the will of the Lord is. An important part of praying is discerning how to pray. Paul instructed in 1 Corinthians 14:15: "I will pray with the spirit, and I will also pray with the understanding" (NKJV). It is understanding our standing—by grace we can come; only by grace can we enter into His presence.

Praying in Jesus' name is to pray with humility and confession. It is praying that the lost will come to Him. It is praying to be more like Jesus—to serve Him more, to love others with the love He shows us. It is getting down to the motives of my heart: Is it as important that God heal my spirit of perfectionism and pride as that He heal my child of retardation?

We can trust that He is a righteous and fair judge and that ultimately His truth will prevail. There are times we simply pray the questions, knowing that He is forging us into His image and that we can trust Him with our lives. John Donne, a poet and preacher of the early 1600s, wrote of welcoming the "battering of our hearts," knowing that when we're in God's hands—in the process—He is making us new:

> Batter my heart, three-personed God, for you
> As yet but knock, breathe, shine, and seek to mend.
> That I may rise and stand, o'erthrow me, and bend
> Your force to break, blow, burn, and make me new.[14]
>
> JOHN DONNE

### Prayer
*Lord, I welcome the forging process You are doing in my life!*
*May I learn of You in amazing, intimate ways in this place!*

The great temptation of the ministry is to celebrate only the presence of Jesus while forgetting his absence. Often the minister is most concerned to make people glad and to create an atmosphere of "I'm okay, you're okay." But in this way everything gets filled up, and there is no empty space left for the affirmation of our basic lack of fulfillment. In this way the presence of Jesus is enforced without connection with his absence. Almost inevitably this leads to artificial joy and superficial happiness. It also leads to disillusionment, because we forget that it is in memory that Jesus Christ is present. If we deny the pain of his absence, we will not be able to taste his sustaining presence either.[15]

HENRI NOUWEN

~ *5* ~

# TIME TO
# TRAVEL LIGHT

*Come to Me, all you who labor and are heavy laden, and I will
give you rest. Take My yoke upon you and learn from Me, for I
am gentle and lowly in heart, and you will find rest for your
souls. For My yoke is easy and My burden is light.*

MATTHEW 11:28-30 NKJV

Autumn told me of the most difficult time of her life. Life was hard for
her and her husband anyway due to their son who had mental problems. But after years of psychiatry, special testing, "tons of prayer,"
and much energy sapped from their marriage and other children,
their twenty-one-year-old son was in prison facing a sentence of
twenty-five years to life. Nothing they had done for him had seemed
to help. Autumn and her husband were devastated; but to make it
even worse, she received a vicious letter from her son in which he
blamed his parents for everything. She said his words were so
drenched in hatred she even feared for their lives if he got out. The letter was her breaking point. How could she go on? What more could
she have done?

Weeping, Autumn walked to a quiet meadow surrounded by trees
and there threw herself on the ground praying, "Try me, Lord! Show
me where I've been wrong or proud. But You take this one. I can't go
on." As she knelt waiting for an answer to the enigma of her son, she

saw a whole area of the meadow covered with a blanket of dewdrops glistening in the sun. It seemed that God spoke to her: "These are all your tears, and I know every one." She began to sob deep, cleansing sobs as she believed in that moment that somehow He cared about her terrible burden. And in that moment, her burden became lighter.

### HE BEARS THE UNBEARABLE

There are times when our prayer concerns are simply too heavy. We are especially vulnerable with our children, because our hearts are so bound up in them. And yet we must pray with a sense of giving them to Him. There have been times I have prayed, "Lord, can't You redeem this situation? I know You can, but will You? Are You?" And even though the unbearable may happen, as in Autumn's situation, we can pray honestly and deeply, releasing the burden into His care. As Autumn related her story, I thought of Oscar Wilde's question: "How else but through a broken heart may Lord Christ enter in?"[16]

I have noticed that there is something very healing about taking Communion when praying for a heavy need, because Communion is a powerful reminder that He bore the unbearable. That is how we can live and pray with an understanding of the easy yoke and light burden.

*You number my wanderings; put my tears into Your bottle;*
*Are they not in Your book? When I cry out to You, Then my*
*enemies will turn back; this I know, because God is for me.*

PSALM 56:8-9 NKJV

## HOW TO PRAY?

There are times we do not even know how to pray. We only know we need rescue! The woman who pressed through the crowd to touch the hem of Jesus' garment knew that Jesus was her last hope. She knew her situation was impossible and desperate, and God met her at her point of need—which is where He meets us. Jack Hayford has said that "prayer is invading the impossible."

It was at Abraham's point of need—his inability to have a son— where God met him and then turned the need into a blessing: Isaac. I have seen this happen in my own family. My mother came to know Christ when she was a lonely single mother. God met her at her need, and her first child, my older sister, definitely is a blessing! She has spent her life as a missionary and raised a beautiful Christian family. It is so true that our Lord redeems all that we place into His hands.

> *All the ways of the LORD are loving and faithful for those who keep the demands of his covenant.*
>
> PSALM 25:10

## TRAVELING LIGHT IN THE MIDST OF LIFE

Last fall Bill and I went with another couple to eastern Oregon. "We're going to see country you've never seen before," our friends promised. "Travel light—wear jeans and bring a warm jacket." We drove east through miles of gently rolling sagebrush, desolate country that vexed the early pioneers. I privately believed I'd already seen the best of Oregon, and, besides, what could be worth seeing in the desert?

Before long we reached Steens Mountain and began driving up a narrow, winding graveled road. We stopped frequently to get out of the car to wonder at the view. Spectacular gorges and sheer cliffs took my breath away as we drove up the side of starkly beautiful, snow-covered hills inhabited by coyotes, deer, birds, mountain goats, and wild horses.

In the distance we saw a sheepherder on a lonely hillside. *What is there about this magnificent land?* I wondered. *It is simply—there.* As we took time to explore the area, we saw that it was difficult terrain, certainly not for the compromised or faint of heart. And for those who chose to live there, the land either made them or broke them. A tenacious few cattle and sheep ranchers seemed to thrive, but we passed many abandoned homesteads, silent witness to those who'd long since moved on to greener pastures.

When we reached the summit of 9,773 feet, we could see both sides of the mountain. Directly east was nearly a mile of sheer vertical drop. On the valley floor below stretched the vast Alvord Desert, characterized by shades of gray and white, signifying alkaline soil. To the west was the green part of Oregon—home—where life waited. We'd planned this getaway as a respite from our busy schedules—a time to reflect, to enjoy our friends, and ponder the future. It had been a hectic, pressure-filled year for all of us, with no end in sight to challenges. I personally felt emotionally and physically tired, not ready for a new year.

I walked around the summit, looking first toward the desert, then toward home, and thought of Scripture I'd just read: "Come to Me, you that labor and are heavy laden, and I will give you rest." I stared at the ruggedly beautiful rock formations, drawn by their beauty and yet put off by the land that seemed to swallow me up. As I stood there, I was reminded of the effect of Jesus' words on my soul—their beauty difficult to comprehend as well. In my life surrounded by family cares and commitments, I long to find His rest—to travel light. But how do I care deeply about needs around me and yet have rest in my soul? Sometimes I want to scream, "Don't tell me this journey is easy or light!" Jesus' words are often easier to take from a distance, filtered away from my heart where they are not so confrontive, so penetrating.

But even as I stubbornly follow, sometimes stumbling, I see that the journey of following Christ takes me to places I never dreamed existed—beautiful places even in their difficulty. And signing up for this journey means I must travel at times on a narrow, infrequently-used road. It may even be an unexpected one in my own backyard. The road sometimes leads to new heights and challenges, to beautiful valleys and still waters. But at times it is lonely and hard. Many of Jesus' disciples followed Him when things were great—when He turned water into wine, when He fed loaves and fish to thousands. But when the message got personal, next to the heart, only a few stuck it out. They complained, "This is a hard teaching. Who can accept it?" (John 6:60).

I can relate to their perplexity. Yet deep inside I know that only Jesus has the words of eternal life. What does it mean to follow Him? For me, it's remembering that I'm not in charge of this journey. Even prayer needs, if we don't continually relinquish them to God, can turn into heavy burdens.[17]

It is possible to pray about the deepest, most complex, and personal needs and yet know that He carries our burdens. How is this possible? Because:

- We can know Him, the object of our trust (see Psalms 27 and 37). He is in today as well as tomorrow, and it's up to us to stay as close to Him as we can and enjoy the journey with Him.

- We can believe that God still moves and changes the unthinkable. His hand is not shortened that He cannot save (see Isa. 59:1; James 5:16; Ps. 32:10-11).

*Prayer*
*Lord, how wonderful to know You care about our deepest*
*prayer burdens. May we give them wholly to You!*


*I Come to You . . .*

*I come to You burdened; I leave You refreshed.*
*I do not understand just how this works;*
    *I only know that it does.*
*As I sat here this morning, as my thoughts swirled*
    *with duties and pressures,*
*I saw only burdens; I knew only pressures. Yet now I feel peace.*
*We have done this before, You and I. Perhaps I am learning.*
    *The pattern seems thus:*
*First I must seek Your silence. I do not talk to You;*
    *nor do I listen.*

*But I am here admitting my frailty and*
  *absorbing Your strength.*
*That is our beginning. Then I pick up one burden, any burden,*
*And hold it up to You. Gingerly I turn it over and around,*
  *looking at it*
  *from every direction.*
*And then I thank You for it, laying it tenderly at Your table,*
*Burden by burden,*
*This job, this child, this hurt, this quandary, this responsibility,*
*And as I pick the last one up, as I turn it over*
  *to examine it before You,*
*I see that it is no longer burdens I have, but gifts.*
*I do not understand how this happens. I only know that it does.*
*I come to You burdened. I leave You refreshed.*
*Thank You, Lord.*

DEANNA HUTCHINGS

~ *6* ~

# TIME TO
# WAIT ON GOD

*Have you not known?*
   *Have you not heard?*
*The everlasting God, the Lord, the Creator of the ends of the earth,*
*Neither faints nor is weary. His understanding is unsearchable.*
   *He gives power to the weak, and to those who have no might*
   *He increases strength.*
*Even the youths shall faint and be weary, and the young men*
   *shall utterly fall,*
*But those who wait on the Lord shall renew their strength;*
*They shall mount up with wings like eagles,*
*They shall run and not be weary, they shall walk and not faint.*

ISAIAH 40:28-31 NKJV

It is hard for me to wait. Even microwave meals take too long to my way of thinking. Sometimes my impatience carries over into my relationship with God, but it's been said that "he who waits for God loses no time." Now as I write this in late winter, it seems as if spring will never come, that winter has been exceptionally long. We here in the Northwest are beginning to grow moss behind our ears (or so it seems). We are waiting for sunshine.

Last fall I said to Bill, "What we need is a good, long, hard winter!" It had been a beautiful late fall Saturday, and we had taken our dogs up an old logging road into the mountains. We were alarmed to see how dry everything was. Creek beds, springs, and waterfalls stood empty, and little puffs of dust arose from our steps as we tried in vain to find water for our dogs to drink. Fortunately we'd brought a jug of water with us, and we sat in a grove of pine trees and ate our lunch and shared our water with the dogs. That's when I made my smart remark about needing winter.

We did get the rain. And the rain continued for days after that, and then it began to snow. The snow would stop for brief periods and then start again. We made lame jokes about putting up flags so we could find each other's houses. And then we had to pay people to shovel off our roofs so they wouldn't collapse. We had a good, hard winter all right—weeks, months of it, but there was nothing to do but "let it snow," as my father used to say.

## TIME TO WAIT

Winter, a resting time for the earth, is a quiet time, a time to wait. Each season is a precursor of the next. Without winter, there would be no spring with its new life, no summer in full bloom, no fall with its harvest. Winter is the time when we ponder what's gone on before. We think about future plantings, what we may do differently. But for this moment, the fields lie fallow. We are suspended in silence. The seed dies, is buried, covered by snow, pelted by rain. There is the sometimes interminable wait for warmth, for sun again, for new growth, for the thaw. For things to move. And even if it does not seem as if the season will ever change—it does.

Paul Tillich wrote of the profound mystery, the tension of waiting on God. He wrote:

> In the psalmist there is an anxious waiting; in the apostle there is a patient waiting. Waiting means not having and having at the same time. . . . A religion in which that is forgotten, no matter how ecstatic or active or reasonable, replaces God by its own creation of an image of God. . . . I think of the theologian who does not wait for God, because he possesses Him, enclosed within a doctrine. I think of the biblical student who does not wait for God, because he possesses Him, enclosed in a book. I think of the churchman who does not wait for God, because he possesses Him, enclosed in an institution. I think of the believer who does not wait for God, because he possesses Him, enclosed within his own experience.
>
> It is not easy to endure this not having God, this waiting for God. . . . It is not easy to proclaim God to children and pagans, to skeptics and secularists, and at the same time to make clear to them that we ourselves do not possess God, that we too wait for Him. I am convinced that much of the rebellion against Christianity is due to the overt or veiled claim of the Christians to possess God, for how can God be possessed? Is God a thing that can be grasped and known among other things? Is God less than a human person? We always have to wait for a human being. Even in the most intimate communion among human beings, there is an element of not having and not knowing, and of waiting.
>
> Therefore, since God is infinitely hidden, free, and incalculable, we must wait for Him in the most absolute and radical way. He is God for us just insofar as we do not possess Him. . . . We have God through not having Him. . . . But the fact

that we wait for something shows that in some way we already possess it.... He who waits in an ultimate sense is not far from that for which he waits.[18]

I can wait on God knowing that He will move; the situation will change just as the seasons change. But how necessary it is to wait on Him, to become still within my spirit—even though I may be in the midst of storms—and know that He is God. As Henri Nouwen describes in *The Way of the Heart*, being silent before God protects the inner fire, the life of the Holy Spirit within me. Coming away to sit at Jesus' feet helps me tend and keep alive the fire of love for Him. And waiting—even in difficult seasons—eventually leads to praise, as John Donne preached: "Prayer and praise is the same thing.... God's house in this world is called the house of prayer, but in heaven it is the house of praise, one even, incessant, and everlasting tenor of thanksgiving.... Prayer properly arises out of the memory of God's mercies, and remembrance informs our prayers."[19]

*Prayer*
*Lord, may I learn what it means to wait patiently for You*
*—and praise You in the midst of it!*

*I waited patiently for the Lord;*
*And He inclined to me, and heard my cry.*
*He also brought me up out of a horrible pit, out of the miry clay,*
*And set my feet upon a rock, and established my steps.*
*He has put a new song in my mouth—praise to our God.*
PSALM 40:1-3 NKJV

*Wait on the Lord; be of good courage, and He shall strengthen your heart; wait, I say, on the Lord.*

PSALM 27:14 NKJV

God does not cease speaking, but the noise of the creatures without, and of our passions within, deafens us, and stops our hearing. We must silence every creature, we must silence ourselves, to hear in the deep hush of the whole soul, the ineffable voice of the spouse. We must bend the ear, because it is a gentle and delicate voice, only heard by those who no longer hear anything else.[20]

FENELON

## Prayer of Praise

*O God, as I change and grow, help me grow toward You. Let me not envy the one who may be planted elsewhere in life or may be in a different season in his or her development. Only let me be faithful where You have me. May I put my roots down deep in Your Word so that I will not be swayed or moved by the storms of life. Thank You for reminding me that I can come freely to You with my most desperate needs—that You redeem all that I place in Your hands.*

*Lord, thank You for reminding me that You can bear the unbearable. May I truly know what it means to know that my burden is light because I am in Your loving hands. I place my cares in You, knowing You care for me. My eyes are ever on You, Lord, and in You I take refuge. Amen.*

*Let nothing trouble or sadden you,*
*All passes, but God does not change,*
*You will conquer all with patience;*
*You lack nothing if God is in your heart,*
*His love is enough.*[21]

TERESA OF AVILA

WAYS TO GROW:
LOOKING BACK TO LOOK FORWARD

Take a moment to reflect on your life this last year. How has God been dealing with you (i.e., reproof, encouragement, discipline, training, etc.)?

- What are you learning about waiting on God?

- Are there any changes—for better or worse—in your relationship with God during this past year? Is there any way you are resisting God by harboring unforgiveness?

*Letting Go*

- If someone has wronged you, write out the "wrong" in detail on a piece of paper. Then pray, "Lord, I give this to You, the perfect judge. I relinquish my hold on this person, this situation. I trust You with the outcome."

- Burn this piece of paper. When you are tempted to relive the offense, remember that it is now in God's hands, not yours. Pray specifically for the person who wronged you and ask God how you may bless him or her.

˷  Read Matthew 7:1-5, Hebrews 12:11-29, and James 3 carefully, thoughtfully. Write in your prayer journal your own response to these verses.

## HOW TO WAIT ON GOD

Before you pray, bow quietly before God and seek to remember and realize who He is, how near He is, how certainly He can and will help.

Just be still before Him and allow His Holy Spirit to waken and stir up in your soul the childlike disposition of absolute dependence and confident expectation.

Wait upon God as a Living Being, as the Living God who notices you and is just longing to fill you with His salvation.

Wait on God till you know you have met Him; prayer will then become so different . . . let there be intervals of silence, reverent stillness of soul, in which you yield yourself to God, in case He may have aught He wishes to teach you or to work in you.

Waiting on Him will become the most blessed part of prayer, and the blessing thus obtained will be doubly precious as the fruit of such fellowship with the Holy One.[22]

ANDREW MURRAY

Behold, Lord, an empty vessel that needs to be filled. My Lord, fill it. I am weak in the faith; strengthen me. I am cold in love; warm me and make me fervent, that my love may go out to my neighbor. I do not have a strong and firm faith; at times I doubt and am unable to trust you altogether. O Lord, help me. Strengthen my faith and trust in you. In you I have sealed the treasure of all I have. I am poor; you are rich and came to be merciful to the poor. I am a sinner; you are upright. With me, there is an abundance of sin; in you is the fullness of righteousness. Therefore I will remain with you, from whom I can receive.

MARTIN LUTHER

Reflections

*Reflections*

_____

_____

_____

_____

_____

_____

_____

_____

_____

_____

_____

_____

_____

_____

_____

_____

_____

_____

_____

_____

_____

_____

_____

# $\mathscr{M}$ATURITY

## DESPERATION DISSOLVES
## INTO LOVE AND PEACE

*Lord, You said You are in the weak, the powerless. Forgive me for attempting to orchestrate, to generate Your message when all You want to do is write Your message on my life. I am willing, Lord—I humbly submit my weak, powerless, and ordinary life into Your hands. May I live my life as a prayer unto You.*

*May I never grow tired of praying for my loved ones, for those around me who need You so much. May I pray that the "Hound of Heaven" will pursue them until they are overcome by Your love. Give my hands strength to do physical tasks, my mind and heart courage to do right and wisdom to see You in all of life. For Yours is the kingdom and the power and the glory forever. Amen.*

When you were younger, you girded yourself and walked where you wished; but when you are old, you will stretch out your hands, and another will gird you and carry you where you do not wish. . . . Follow Me.

JOHN 21:18-19 NKJV

# *Four*

# EFFECTIVE PRAYERS
# FROM AN EFFECTIVE LIFE

⟡

*The righteous will flourish like a palm tree; they will grow like a*
*cedar of Lebanon; planted in the house of the LORD, they will*
*flourish in the courts of our God. They will still bear fruit in old*
*age, they will stay fresh and green.*

PSALM 92:12-14

⟡

In the fourth and final painting of Thomas Cole's *Journey of Life* series, we see an old man gliding serenely toward the end of his trip on the river. It is twilight, and a sense of peace pervades the scene. The picture reminds me of the spiritual passage of maturity in which Jesus promises us His peace, and we will not be afraid because He will be with us always. His peace does not necessarily mean an end to troubles or worries; it does mean we can pray effectively in the midst of them because we know our Source.

Are there fears at this place of maturity? Of course. Just because one is all grown up does not mean one does not have fears. There is the very real fear of being alone and forgotten. How we need to know again, as in the beginning, that He is near, intimately near—maybe not with a lot of instructions or teaching, but this time just offering His presence.

Spiritual maturity takes us back full circle, to coming to Him as a child—not as a spoiled, demanding child, but as a trusting, obedient one. God does intend for us to grow up, and our prayer lives will reflect it.

In our youth-conscious society, we resist maturity. The writer of Ecclesiastes describes the ambivalence of maturity:

> Someday the light of the sun and the moon and the stars will all seem dim to you. Rain clouds will remain over your head. Your body will grow feeble, your teeth will decay, and your eyesight fail. The noisy grinding of grain will be shut out by your deaf ears, but even the song of a bird will keep you awake. You will be afraid to climb up a hill or walk down a road. Your hair will turn as white as almond blossoms. You will feel lifeless and drag along like an old grasshopper.
>
> ECCLESIASTES 12:2-5 CEV

Doesn't sound too appealing, does it? It's all too painfully true to many of us, so we joke about it and buy funny cards to make us feel better. We might as well.

As Barbara Johnson says, this is the stage where we start choosing our cereal for the fiber, not the toy. My body is reminding me that life does not stay the same, that we are on a continuum through time. But there's a positive side to maturity—experience and wisdom, often purchased at great price. And spiritual maturity is where we want to be, after all is said and done.

## MY LIFE AS A PRAYER

What should our prayer lives look like as they mature? When we grow up in Him, we hope that we begin to "look" more like Him. We can measure our growth by asking ourselves these questions:

- Am I more like Jesus?

- Does my life make it easier for others to come to know Him?

- Is my spiritual life natural (not super-spiritual or religious)?

- Do I go out of my way when the Spirit directs me to pray and care for people?

- Do I have time for the kind of people Jesus had time for?

- Do I pray without ceasing and with thanksgiving?

~ *1* ~

## MATURITY
## MEANS OBEDIENCE

*What is needed in spiritual matters is reckless abandonment to*
*the Lord Jesus Christ, reckless and uncalculating abandonment,*
*with no reserve anywhere about it; not sad—you cannot be sad*
*if you are abandoned absolutely. . . . One life yielded to God at*
*all costs is worth thousands only touched by God.*[1]

OSWALD CHAMBERS

Maturity is a place to keep saying, "Yes, Lord."

There is a poignant illustration of what it means to enter spiritual maturity in John chapter 21. It was after the cross, after the Resurrection. The disciples had gone fishing and were out all night with no success. Jesus appeared to them on the seashore with a fire going. He was baking bread in the hot coals, and He called to them to throw their nets over on the other side of the boat. They did so, and soon they were swamped with a huge catch. They hauled the fish ashore, and Jesus tenderly fixed breakfast for His hungry disciples, most of whom had recently abandoned Him in His hour of greatest need. Jesus asked Peter penetrating questions: "Peter, do you love me?" Three times Jesus asked him, and three times Peter insisted, "Yes, Lord, You know I love You!" Then Jesus gave some insight to Peter as to what it meant to follow Him: "Someday you will be led where you don't want to go." He was talking to Peter about the cost of following Him, of obedience.

Maturity is a paradox. It often means we have less control over what happens in our lives (and what a pity—we have so much insight as to what *should* happen!); but if we allow Him to, God has more and more control. This fact was illustrated to me again just this morning. I thought I had three prime hours to write, with no interruptions. I was going full-tilt on my computer, writing deep spiritual thoughts when the phone rang, and there was an errand I had to immediately run. It couldn't wait. I dressed, got in the car, and did it, consoling myself that I had at least two hours left.

My errand done, I came back and began to work again. Just then Sam, our yellow lab, came into my office and put his paw up on my lap, begging to be let out. So what am I to do? Amy was at school, and Bill was at a meeting, so I went out in the yard with Sam. The first thing he saw were three deer and immediately began to chase them as if his life depended on it. I finally corralled him, not too happy with my furry friend, and again went back to the computer, my time having now dwindled to an hour.

This is a very mundane example, but it's an illustration of how much I am *not* in control! I've found I must live as unto Jesus, responding to others as unto Him, trusting Him with the ultimate outcome. Rarely do things turn out exactly the way we want them to, and just when we think everything is going the way it should, it can change.

I think of a young couple I know who were planning to adopt a baby and were overjoyed when tiny newborn Leah was placed into their arms and hearts—only to have the birth mother change her mind a few weeks later. Heartbroken, they still do not understand why it happened the way it did, but they are trusting that God is in control and has a plan and purpose for their family. Life is often a series of painful interruptions and intrusions. Life can be messy.

Seasons remind us, however, that we can grow; we can change. We can get better . . . and maturity is better. Youth is a wonderful time of idealism when we live mainly on hopes and dreams, and nothing seems impossible. Then some of us go through a time of invincibility—when we're sure that if we follow a certain formula, we will succeed. But as we know, life happens. The other day I listened to a friend who is having a crisis in her family, and I was again reminded that it rains on the just and the unjust. Sometimes things happen with no apparent explanation. She'd done it all "right," yet she is now praying fervently for God's intervention.

Growing up in the Lord is finally having the courage to pray big prayers because we're able to see the big picture. We become consumed by His love—so consumed that we become His hands extended, and we begin to see with His eyes. A. W. Tozer wrote in *The Pursuit of God*:

> The way to deeper knowledge of God is through the lonely valleys of soul poverty. . . . The blessed ones who possess the Kingdom are they who have repudiated every external thing and have rooted from their hearts all sense of possessing. These are the "poor in spirit." . . . These blessed poor are no longer slaves to the tyranny of things. They have broken the yoke of the oppressor; and this they have done not by fighting

but by surrendering. Though free from all sense of possessing, they yet possess all things. "Theirs is the kingdom of heaven."[2]

## SURRENDER

Surrender does not always bring with it lyrical highs and enthusiastic feelings. Some who have gone through such experiences may give testimonies of joy and appreciation, but their accounts seem nontransferable. Each of us must make our own surrender, in circumstances that seem to be unique.[3]

EMILIE GRIFFIN

There is a cost to serving Jesus, as Dietrich Bonhoeffer, a German pastor involved in the resistance to the Nazis, wrote in *The Cost of Discipleship.* He wrote these words from a Nazi camp where he was imprisoned: "When Christ calls a man, He bids him come and die."[4] Such words carry weight when we know that, just as the Allies were liberating Europe, Dietrich was stripped naked by his captors and hanged.

Now when we seem to be able to have it all, the gospel of obedience isn't that popular, and yet it is true more than ever. There are times when it is not convenient, pleasant, or easy to serve God. Many Christians in the world are facing persecution and death, even as I write this, just for being Christians. And yet our American culture is invasive; our comforts and indulgences can kill us, spiritually speaking. Henry Blackaby writes, "Understanding what God is about to do where you are is more important than telling God what you want to do for Him. God hasn't told us to go away and do some work for Him. He has told us that He is already at work trying to bring a lost world to Himself. If we will adjust our lives to Him in a love relationship, He will show us where He is at work."[5]

What do I really know about obedience, about following Christ? Very little. But I want to know more. Last fall I had barely gotten myself home when I had to leave again to do a retreat in southern California. I am trying to guard against being overcommitted, for the sake of my family and my health. But leaving home this particular Friday morning was especially tough, as I felt that "my soul hadn't caught up with my body." I was thinking, *What on earth am I doing? I need to be home. How can I ever share anything meaningful with these people?* as I was on my way to the airport. That old familiar feeling of utter homesickness washed over me, as it often does when I leave home. I turned on the CD player in my car, and a gentle song about what it meant to follow Jesus filled the car. The words were riveting:

*To be ever in His presence,*
*Where He leads me, I will go.*[6]

It suddenly occurred to me. *Of course. This is a small taste of what it means to obey, to deny myself so that I may be in His presence. Obedience is just being with Jesus, wherever that takes me.* The instant I recognized it, I had a sense of joy—I was walking in obedience to the Lord! The point is, there is a cost to following Jesus, a cost to obedience, even in its joys and satisfaction. We may find ourselves going places and doing things we'd rather not do. Leaving home is a small cost to me compared to what many are experiencing. And yet the prize is His presence, a wonderful reality.

Richard Foster writes, "Joy is not found in singing a particular kind of music or in getting with the right kind of group or even in exercising the charismatic gifts of the Spirit, good as all these may be. Joy is found in obedience. When the power that is in Jesus reaches into our work and play and redeems them, there will be joy where once there was mourning. To overlook this is to miss the meaning of the Incarnation."[7]

> I want my life, Lord, to be an answer for your love for me: my actions and my words, my thoughts and my dreams—all a response to the great reality of your presence in Jesus, that calls into question my selfishness and my pride. Amen.[8]

EUGENE PETERSEN

*Prayer*
*Lord, may I obey You*
*quickly, joyfully!*

~ *2* ~

## MATURITY MEANS GENEROUS PRAYER FOR OTHERS

*Those who sow in tears will reap with songs of joy. He who goes out weeping, carrying seed to sow, will return with songs of joy, carrying sheaves with him.*

PSALM 126:5-6

During the time of the French Revolution, the aristocracy were being hauled by the cartful to the guillotine. It got so that executions were expected, routine. But one woman was not willing to go meekly. She wailed and cried and protested so heartrendingly along the road that onlookers who'd grown used to the dignity of the royalty submitting to the inevitable were shocked and sobered. They suddenly were ashamed of what they were doing.[9]

Perhaps we need more passionate prayer warriors who will not just accept the status quo of our society. The prison population (mostly young people) has *doubled* in the last twenty years. Teen suicide is high. Abortion is a fact of life. Drug, alcohol, and gambling addictions are destroying the potential of young people. We have grown numb to the effects of sin in our culture, and we watch people rush like lemmings to the sea on their way to destruction. We become so conditioned to having our moral senses assaulted that we may inwardly shrug, thinking, *This is just the way it is now.*

But thank God for the many who are praying not only for their own concerns but for other concerns as well, rising up to cry, "Enough!" Individuals, organizations such as Moms in Touch, and many other prayer movements are committed to praying for a revival. It is one thing to pray for our own children—and Bill and I believe we are called to do just that—but we must pray for needs around us, too. James 5:16 says, "The effective, fervent prayer of a righteous man avails much" (NKJV).

Dr. J. Edwin Orr, after a study of revivals in history, said that all revivals from Christ's time to ours have come when one to eleven people got completely right with God and then prayed extraordinary prayers.[10]

## FASTING

Fasting is an important part of prayer, and I have seen benefits many times when a situation called for fasting. In our early days of publishing magazines, we often had days of fasting and prayer for God's direction. Bill and I have fasted and prayed for our children on occasion. I find it helpful to "fast" occasionally from watching TV or listening to the radio.

Fasting is not a form of manipulating God; it helps us focus in more clearly on how to pray. As Elmer Towns in *Fasting for Spiritual Breakthrough* writes: "We fast and pray for results, but the results are in God's hands. One of the greatest spiritual benefits of fasting is becoming more attentive to God—becoming more aware of our own inadequacies and His adequacy, our own contingencies and His self-sufficiency—and listening to what He wants us to be and do."[11]

Towns goes on to describe the different kinds of fasts that we can rediscover today to help us focus on specific areas of prayer needs, and I highly recommend his very helpful book. Particularly in our society of indulgence and "noise," fasting is a valuable spiritual discipline.

*God answers prayer.* If there is one theme played throughout Scripture, *it is that He is the Redeemer and redeems all that we place in His hand*—our lives, situations, and people. How good to know that all that we commit to Him is safe.

*Prayer*
*Lord, may we be people who care,*
*who pray with intensity and compassion*
*to see the lost come to You!*

~ *3* ~

## MATURITY
### LEADS TO PRAISE

*Enter into His gates with thanksgiving,*
*And into His courts with praise.*
*Be thankful to Him, and bless His name.*

PSALM 100: 5 NKJV

*Oh, that men would give thanks to the Lord for His goodness,*
*And for His wonderful works to the children of men!*
*For He satisfies the longing soul, and fills the hungry soul*
*with goodness.*

PSALM 107:8-9 NKJV

Living with a spirit of praise is a wonderful symptom of spiritual maturity. One late February afternoon I'd been working long and hard at my computer and needed to get out of the house. Although we live near the mountains, we cannot see them from our house, as we're surrounded by trees. To see the mountains, I must walk to the meadow.

I was not only tired of the weather, but my life itself seemed dreary—stagnant, boring—almost as if someone had hit the "pause" button, and I was at a plateau. The travel section in the Sunday paper was filled with descriptions of exotic, faraway places that sounded wonderful. I was ready to see a new view of life, a new country. But today a trip to the meadow would have to do.

I put on my jacket and gloves and tromped through the trees, hurrying before it got dark. The air held just the hint of a thaw, and I heard the sound of an early red-winged blackbird. Before long I reached the meadow, and, sure enough, there were the mountains. I stopped and caught my breath. The still breathtakingly blue sky was spectacular with the sun setting on the great billowing clouds and the mountains. The brilliant colors of purple and silver and white were like an artist's exotic palette.

I stopped and simply took in the view. "Thank You," I breathed. "Thank You." How wonderful it was to savor God's world, His presence. I thought of the psalmist's description: "Clouds and darkness surround Him; Righteousness and justice are the foundation of His throne. . . . The heavens declare His righteousness, and all the peoples see His glory" (Ps. 97:2, 6 NKJV).

As is my habit when I walk, I prayed. I automatically began to pray again for a need that had been bothering me for some time, and then I stopped. This time instead of pleading and petitioning God as I usually did, I began to praise Him for His perfect answer. And my petty discontent and concerns seemed to fade in His presence and in the light of His magnificent creation.

Suddenly the birds, which had seemed quite incidental before my walk, now seemed the important thing, and I was amazed to see tiny buds on a willow tree. I was reminded of Jesus' words: "Look at the birds of the air . . . your heavenly Father feeds them. Are you not of more value than they?" (Matt. 6:26 NKJV). As I slowly walked through the meadow, I was aware that my depression had lifted.

What had changed? Nothing—and everything. My life had the

same needs, the same situation, and yet it was new because, as I held up my life to Him in praise, I was in a new place.

Genesis 29:31-35 tells the story of Leah, wife of Jacob. She was sure that if she bore Jacob sons, he would love her, but he didn't. He loved Rachel instead. What a sad, dreary place for someone to be—unloved and unwanted. Finally after the birth of her fourth son, Leah said, "Now I will praise the Lord." Her situation hadn't changed because Jacob still did not love her, and yet it had—because of the dynamic of praise. Leah made up her mind that she would praise God from where she was, and she had a fruitful life.

Learning to praise Him in all things is a dynamic that is changing my life. I wish it hadn't taken me so long to learn this incredible secret, but the concept of living continually in a spirit of praise and worship can seem as far away as a Caribbean island. It sounds wonderful, but how do I get there from here?

It is one thing to come to church to sing the praise songs, but it is another to *live* with an attitude of praise and worship. I've found that cultivating this attitude is simple and yet profound. Deuteronomy 30:14 says, "The word is very near you; it is in your mouth and in your heart so you may obey it." Praise comes from an honest heart of obedience, from recognition of God's powerful presence, and from faith that He cares for me. Not that everything is always hunky-dory. It is, after all, a *sacrifice* of praise that we bring. God is worthy of our praise, because if there is anything we know about Him, it is that He is the Redeemer—He redeems all things. And He is faithful. How can we *not* praise Him? We can get a fresh perspective of life when we simply make up our minds to praise Him regardless of circumstances.[12]

Yoka Wilcott told me: "On November 15, 1998, we got the phone call all parents dread. My two older sons were in a head-on car accident, and we rushed to the hospital where we'd been told the boys had been taken. We waited and finally learned that one was sent to another hospital, and the other son was life-flighted to yet another facility. Our son who was life-flighted was in very bad shape, and we didn't see him for six hours. In the awful hours when we didn't really know what was going on, all I could do was lift my sons to God. When I saw my oldest son for the first time in ICU, nothing could prepare me for what I saw, and I was brokenhearted. We gathered in a prayer circle, and I was filled with an amazing peace as we surrendered all to Him. God's Word became alive to me, and I began to sing songs of praise and deliverance. God began to show me that He was in control. I was totally helpless to know how to fix my children's pain, but peace came as I released my sons to God."

> Eternal Father of my soul, let my first thought today be of You, let my first impulse be to worship You, let my first speech be Your name, let my first action be to kneel in prayer. Amen.[13]
>
> JOHN BAILLE

## GO WHERE PRAISE IS

It takes a conscious effort, an act of obedience to praise Him. And although we may not be able to praise God *for* something, we can praise Him *in* it. Praise is a new way of thinking, of praying. Not long ago Bill and I visited Ellis Island in New York harbor where many immigrants entered this country. I was captivated by their stories. Many of them left everything—their parents, their native land and tongue to come to a new place with only a trunk of belongings and great expectations. They made a deliberate choice to go to a country with new customs, a new language, and a new currency.

Choosing to live a life of praise is like that. It means coming to God with only myself and great expectations of who He is and what He can do with what I offer Him. It takes a deliberate act of my will, like my being drawn to the meadow that February afternoon. I went because I had expectations of seeing the mountains. I didn't really feel like going, and yet I went there to see the big picture, to lift me out of myself, my narrow confines. So it is with being in God's presence through praise. His presence is so encompassing, His dreams and plans far beyond anything I can imagine. How wonderful to know that I can be in the midst of life *with Him* as praise continually fills my heart and mind and mouth. "I will bless the Lord at all times," David sang. "His praise shall continually be in my mouth" (Ps. 34:1 KJV).

The Psalms are full of praises to God. Choose a psalm or two, such as 103 and 104, and from these two psalms list things for which you can praise the Lord. Try incorporating into your personal devotions the singing of a hymn or praise song, or even write one yourself.

*Praise to the Lord! O let all that is in me adore Him!*
*All that hath life and breath, come now with praises before Him!*
*Let the Amen sound from His people again:*
*Gladly for aye we adore Him!*[14]

I will thank [God] for the pleasures given me through my senses, for the glory of the thunder, for the mystery of music, the singing of the birds and the laughter of children. . . . Truly, O Lord, the earth is full of thy riches![15]

EDWARD KING

*Prayer*
*Lord, I want praise for You*
*to saturate my prayer life!*

~ *4* ~

## MATURITY MEANS
## TO LOVE AND SERVE

*By this all men will know that you are my disciples, if you love
one another.*

JOHN 13:35

*Dear friends, let us love one another, for love comes from God.
Everyone who loves has been born of God and knows God.
Whoever does not love does not know God.*

1 JOHN 4:7

Not long ago I had a dream. I was making breakfast for three people,
one of them a man in the community I know only casually. He'd made
a remark to me some time ago about my daughter, something I considered racist and condescending. I'd seethed with hidden anger,
vowing never to speak to him again. There was another man in my
dream, a Christian brother with whom we'd had a disagreement. And
then there was a woman in my dream that I only know from televi-
sion, a woman I regarded as *awful*. Why breakfast for those three—
all so different?

In my dream I was buzzing around, trying to serve up the best
breakfast I could, but I kept getting interrupted, stumbling over
things as I doggedly prepared this meal. The three stood silently waiting, and somehow I knew they were hungry, and I just needed to serve
them, but it seemed so difficult.

I awoke, wondering, and realized these were people I needed to forgive—all for different reasons—and not only to forgive, but also to love and serve.

When Jesus made breakfast on the seashore for His disciples after they'd forsaken and denied Him, there was something healing, poignant in the gesture. It was forgiveness, but it was more than that. It was grace and mercy offered in a spirit of love and service.

Real maturity may not be so much that we have more of Jesus, but that He has more of us so that we can love and serve those He places in our lives the way He would. Perhaps it is only when we reach real maturity in Christ that we truly are able to give our whole selves away, catching a glimpse of what true love means.

> *Measure thy life by loss instead of gain;*
> *Not by the wine drunk, but the wine poured forth;*
> *For love's strength standeth in love's sacrifice;*
> *And whoso suffers most hath most to give.*[16]
>
> MRS. HAMILTON KING

*Prayer*
*O Lord, how little do I know what it means*
*to love as You do. Please teach me!*

An unknown writer penned these thoughts:

I was a revolutionary when I was young, and all my prayer to God was: "Lord, give me the energy to change the world."

As I approached middle age and realized that my life was

half gone without my changing a single soul, I changed my prayer to: "Lord, give me the grace to change all those who come into contact with me, just my family and friends, and I shall be satisfied."

Now that I am an old man and my days are numbered, my prayer is: "Lord, give me the grace to change myself."

~ *5* ~

## MATURITY MEANS
## BEARING FRUIT

*As each one has received a gift, minister it to one another, as
good stewards of the manifold grace of God. If anyone speaks, let
him speak as the oracles of God. If anyone ministers, let him do
it as with the ability which God supplies.*

1 PETER 4:10-11 NKJV

*If you want to love Him better now while you are here, trust Him.
The more you trust Him, the better you will love Him. If you ask,
"How shall I trust Him?" I answer, "Try Him. The more you
make trial of Him, the more your trust in Him will be
strengthened."*

UNKNOWN

Bearing fruit means that it becomes evident to others that God is at
work in our lives. Fruit is a desirable and natural consequence of
maturity. Many times I look at my world and pray, "Lord, how can I
ever bear fruit for You from my life?"

I saw it clearly in my father's life many years ago. When I was very
small, one of the old bachelors, Ben, who lived in a shack not far from
our home in Montana, was too sick to get out of bed. Mother prepared
some food, and I tagged along with Dad as he took it to Ben. I followed
Dad into Ben's dirty one-room shack that smelled so badly I could
hardly breathe and watched Dad fix a plate of food and gently prop

Ben up to eat, placing a generous slice of mother's pie on the side for later. Dad didn't say much, other than a comment or two about the weather. And then I *knew*—as I saw Dad tenderly place his work-worn hand on Ben's shoulder and briefly pray that Ben would feel better—that as surely as Dad brought that warm meal, he brought Jesus, too. The little shack seemed to glow with His presence. My father did quiet acts of love like this all the time; it was just an outgrowth of his life. It was simple, natural. It was profound.

Obedience and submission to God is what produces fruit from our lives. It may mean being inconvenienced out of love for God and others and a simple life of love and service out of which happiness—like an inner well of water—overflows. It may mean being willing to speak and say the things I must out of brokenness rather than giving pat answers and formulas. It means being real and having time for people.

Years ago a neighbor of mine told me, "You're always dressed up, and you're always going to church." Her comment stunned me as I realized it was true. My life certainly wasn't bearing fruit, and as far as she could tell, I may as well have been a mannequin. Real ministry and fruit come out of brokenness, and the Holy Spirit must shape my life in order for the message to be heard. It is only when His Word, as the prophet Jeremiah wrote, is "in my heart like a burning fire" (20:9) that it becomes real to others.

There have been other times when I've seen Jesus through others' lives—a compassionate friend who offered just the insight I needed to hear, the prayer of a pastor when I was sick, straight and

loving truth from my family. They gave unaware, a natural outflow-
ing of God from their lives. But they brought a sense of Him to me,
directing me always to the Word and the only real source of comfort,
peace, and joy.

I will never forget years ago being at a very busy booksellers'
convention and having a chance conversation with a woman I'd just
met. She heard between the lines of our conversation my frustration
of wanting to be a writer and also my desire to give my family first
priority. She came back later where I was and asked, "Can I pray
with you?" She prayed simply but with great wisdom, and although
I have not seen her since, through the years her prayer has often
comforted and directed me. God used her in my life, and I am
grateful.

Prayer is so intimate that we may be reluctant to "intrude" on
someone's life to offer it. Yet most people welcome our offering of
prayer—and it could be life-changing for someone.

### Prayer
*O Lord, may I have time for the people that You bring to me!*

The one who has had but little trouble in life is not a particularly helpful person. But one who has gone through a hundred
and one trials, experiences, deaths, blasted hopes, shocks,
and a tragedy or two and has learned his lesson. . . . Such a person is worthwhile. He is able to enter into the need of suffer-
ing humanity and pray it through. He can enter into perfect
fellowship with a person who is in unspoken agony of spirit

and pressure of trial. He is able to look beyond the frailty of flesh and, remembering we are but dust, to trust God with a sublime faith for victory and power. Do not be afraid of the process. I see such rich possibilities in it all. We long to be of service to needy mankind. Nothing can better equip us than to break in spirit and heart and so become clear, sparkling wine, rich and refreshing.[17]

J. W. FOLLETTE

~ *6* ~

## MATURITY MEANS COMING
## ONCE AGAIN AS A CHILD

*May my life be a continual prayer, a long act of love. May noth-
ing distract me from You, neither noise nor diversions. O my
Master, I would so love to live with You in silence. But what I love
above all is to do Your will, and since You want me to still
remain in the world, I submit with all my heart for love of You.
I offer You the cell of my heart; may it be Your little Bethany.
Come rest there; I love You so.[18]*

BLESSED ELIZABETH OF THE TRINITY

I confess, I miss having a house full of noisy children. I'm thankful
that we are entering the grandchildren era, and we are ready. There is
just something wonderful about children. Last summer we had Bill's
parents for two weeks. Then another couple we consider our spiritual
parents, Dorothy and Earl Book, spent some days with us.
Juxtapositioned between these visits were two visits from Will, our
year-old grandbaby. I could see the similarities in infancy and age:

↶ We needed those naps! Regular nutritious meals were important.

↶ We learned that it's best to walk more slowly and appreciate things
   close to home—the birds, the squirrels, the deer.

↶ We did things all day, and at the end of the day I wasn't sure what
   we'd done. We just "hung out." We talked, we played. It was won-

derful. We simply enjoyed each other and enjoyed life—and that is how we can enjoy God.

Maturity can bring us back to a sense of childlike wonder again. In the midst of not knowing what lies ahead, we can have a sense of trust. Emerson wrote, "All I have seen teaches me to trust the Creator for all I have not seen." God's very nature is faithfulness, and He cannot deny Himself. Trusting Him *not knowing* is an opportunity for my roots to go down deep, down where the nourishment is, to His Word, which is faithful and true. The more we learn about prayer, the more we learn how natural a part of life it is. The world can be overwhelming, but a relationship with a loving Father God through prayer is inexpressible comfort.

Ruth Lovegren, a dear friend of ours, recently lost her husband, Ken. After working hard for many years running a resort, Ken and Ruth were getting ready to retire and enjoy some traveling when Ken was taken with a sudden heart attack. Later after the funeral, friends and family had gone home, and Ruth was left with a terrible void deep within, a desperate, empty feeling. She said that for the first time in her life, she understood how a person would turn to drink or drugs or contemplate suicide. The anguish was unbearable.

One night she prayed with many tears, "God, I would never do those things because I have You, but somehow You must fill this void. I cannot go on like this." While she was sobbing, her daughter phoned, and Ruth said, "Ann, I can't talk right now."

Her daughter responded, "Okay, Mom, but I'm going to pray."

Ruth said that by the time she went to bed, she realized that the desperate, aching void was gone. Yes, she's still lonely; she still misses Ken, but God met her in her most desperate moment, reminding her that He was there. Ruth is a wonderful blessing to Bill and me and is on our ministry board. Several times a year she travels with me on speaking engagements. Her wisdom and insights are encouraging many. Although God has a different plan for Ruth in her retirement than she had expected, He is using her in a beautiful way in ministering to her large extended family and community and to people like me.

What is His message to us in this place of maturity? Simply that we must not cast away our confidence, that when He begins a work in us, He will finish it. We must simply stay with Him, knowing His plans for us are good.

FINISHING WELL

How good it is to finish well! In the book *Into Thin Air* Jon Krakauer tells of the Mt. Everest climb that ended in disaster. He also wrote about other mountain-climbing expeditions in *Into the Wild*. He made the point that often accidents and disasters happen on the *descent*— toward the end of the journey. Then we can get tired and perhaps become a little reckless and coast on our past successes.

Compare the life of Solomon to the life of Daniel—Solomon had every potential to end his life in greatness; instead his heart was turned away from God. Daniel lived a fruitful life—living his entire life for God. The same could be said for Joseph as well. Although he was rewarded by much success and prestige in his adulthood, his heart stayed true to God. Maturity for the life of the believer should be the most fruitful time, but there are temptations here, too. How essential it is to stay honest and humble and centered on God's Word.

There is much opportunity at this place in life to pray effectively, now having wisdom and a clearer perspective. In our information age, we know that believers in some parts of the world face persecution, even death, and we can faithfully pray for them. Yet our own culture is subtly, pervasively hostile to righteousness, and the lure of the world is strong, its messages persistent.

Shortly after my father died, Mother gave me a black-and-white snapshot of Dad holding me when I was two years old. I cherish that picture, as there is something infinitely precious about being held by one's father.

Being rooted in God is like being held by Him. As we look to the future, we have no idea what's ahead. For now it's enough to trust Him so that we can bear fruit, can flourish always—no matter what's going on around us. We can cling to Him when we think we understand, and especially when we know we don't, knowing that He holds us and all that we commit to Him.

True maturity in God leads us to pray with trust in who He is—taking us back full circle to the Abba Father, to knowing we are held, that our lives are in His hands.

We can be *planted* in God: "Blessed is the man who walks not in the counsel of the ungodly, nor stands in the path of sinners, nor sits in the seat of the scornful; but his delight is in the law of the Lord, and in His law he meditates day and night. He shall be like a tree planted by the rivers of water that brings forth its fruit in its season, whose leaf also shall not wither; and whatever he does shall prosper" (Ps. 1:1-3 NKJV).

*What is your life giving birth to? My life?*

As God's offspring, our lives also give birth. We have purpose. As we stay in Him, we begin to look more like Him. We also will be able to reproduce spiritually.

Do we look like our Father? Is there a growing family resemblance? The resemblance may not be so noticeable right at first. But the more time we spend with Him—the more we become doers of the Word and not hearers only—the more we will be like Him. Sometimes it takes awhile to look like our Father. We must ask ourselves, "Is His story being written so deeply upon my life that others know I belong to Him? Does my life make others want to know Him?"

Do those around me want what I have? Does my life make it *easier* for others to come to know Him? Religion kills, but relationship brings life. The most important relationship any of us will have in life is with God—and prayer is a consequence of that relationship. If Jesus, God's Son, needed to come away frequently to quiet places to talk to His Father, how much more do we need it? We cannot give out of what we do not have. We must ask the question: "What lies within me that others want?" Prayer is almighty God helping us to give ourselves back to Him. Henri Nouwen asks the provocative question:

"The question is not: How many people take you seriously? How much are you going to accomplish? Can you show some results? But: Are you in love with Jesus?"[19]

*We can take others with us into our prayer.*

Some time ago we had an exchange student living with us. Dorli was a university student from Austria, a very attractive and intelligent young woman with little religious background. We were eager to share our faith with her. We took her to our church. We gave her Christian literature and books, but nothing seemed to connect.

One evening our family was at one of our son's basketball games. The high school gym where he was playing was close to a hospital where a good friend of mine lay critically ill. At halftime I thought I would run up to the hospital and briefly pray with her. Dorli wanted to go with me, so we went up to my friend's darkened room, and I gave her a hug, smoothed her hair back from her face, and held her hand as I prayed very simply, very briefly for her. Then Dorli and I went back to the noisy game to see if Andy's team would win.

Several days later as Dorli was getting ready to go back to Austria, she came into my room to talk to me. Hesitantly she asked, "When you prayed with your sick friend the other night, how did you do that? Will you teach me how? Can I just talk to God like that?"

I was astounded—but she had seen the "treasure" of God's presence shining through my ordinary, imperfect life! I assured her, "Yes, it is that simple. You can talk to God."

*Prayer*
*O Lord, You have given me so much!*
*May my prayer life be a reflection of Your goodness!*

## Prayer of Praise

*Lord, I do not say, "Be with me," for of course You are! I say, "Open my eyes to Your Presence." I praise You for Your faithfulness and mercies that You offer new every morning. Thank You for showing me that I do not have to generate answers—I simply must stay plugged into You, the true vine.*

*Increase my vision, Lord. May I not be content with the status quo, but may I freely share with others what You have given me. Lord, give me grace to learn the joys of obedience. And may I rehearse Your amazing goodness continually! Amen.*

### WAYS TO GROW: ASSESSMENT

Prayerfully consider these questions:

- At this place of maturity, is my relationship with God deepening or growing colder?

- Where do I feel I can grow?

- Am I willing to be obedient to Him, regardless of where He leads?

- Am I praying with worship or worry?

- For fresh insights on ministry, read 1 Peter 4 and 5, 2 Peter, and 1

John. Think back to a time when someone ministered to you. Prayerfully watch for ways you can minister to others—and be open to surprises!

↝ Ask yourself, "Is Christ so thoroughly at home with me that my presence brings a sense of *Him* to others?"

↝ Surrender to Jesus Christ is individual, personal. Pray for a heart willing to give all to Jesus and make Him Lord. Read Madame Guyon's statement about what it means to abandon oneself to God:

Courage, dear soul. You have come to the edge of the Red Sea, where soon you will see the enemy receive his reward. Follow on your present path. Remain immovable, like a rock. Do not find a pretext to stir from where you are. . . . The Lord will fight for you now. Many people break down at this place. They do not find the way out. They stop here and never advance. . . . That which is a rock of destruction to others is the port of safety to such a one. . . . You must know that in all the many states that are involved in the interior life, each new stage, each new level, is preceded by a *sacrifice*. Then comes an *abandon*, and following that is always a state of utter *destitution*. . . . *Abandoned ones are praising ones.*[20]

MADAME GUYON

*Make your own prayer journal.*

↝ Tailor-make your own prayer journal, a private project between you and God. Take care not to get too fancy or elaborate, as it may tend to make your prayers more guarded and careful. Get a simple spiral notebook and keep it close to your Bible. You want something ordinary in which you can pour out your prayers and thoughts uninhibitedly.

꜠ Record the date at the top of the page, your prayer, and perhaps a Scripture you are pondering. Or you may prefer to keep a separate page for each specific need, with the name of the individual you are praying for at the top of each page. Record a Scripture or prayer for that specific person. Leave blank space to record other prayers or answers to prayer later.

Allow the spirit of God to dwell within you; then in his love he will come and make a habitation with you; he will reside in you and live in you.

Set off on the path of prayer with confidence; then swiftly and speedily will you reach the place of peace, which is your stronghold against the place of fear.[21]

EVAGRIUS OF PONTUS

*Reflections*

_____

_____

_____

_____

_____

_____

_____

_____

_____

_____

_____

_____

_____

_____

_____

_____

_____

_____

_____

_____

_____

_____

_____

_____

_____

_____

## *Reflections*

_____

_____

_____

_____

_____

_____

_____

_____

_____

_____

_____

_____

_____

_____

_____

_____

_____

_____

_____

_____

_____

_____

_____

_____

_____

# OTES

## INTRODUCTION

1 Simon Tugwell, O.P., *Ways of Imperfection* (Springfield, Ill., Templegate Publishers, 1985).

2 Grace A. Brame, Introduction to Evelyn Underhill's *Ways of the Spirit* (New York: Crossroad, 1996), 20.

3 Andrew Murray, *Waiting on God* (London: Nisbet & Co., Ltd., 1895).

4 Richard Foster, *Prayer: Finding the Heart's True Home* (San Francisco: Harper San Francisco, 1992), 8.

## INFANCY

### WHAT DO I NEED?

1 Oswald Chambers, *The Best from All His Books*, ed. Harry VerPloegh (Nashville: Oliver Nelson, 1989), 210.

2 Calvin Miller, *Walking with Saints* (Nashville: Thomas Nelson, 1995), 121-122.

3 *Teresa of Avila: A Life of Prayer*, Classics of Faith & Devotion (Portland, Ore.: Multnomah Press, 1983), 125.

4 A. W. Tozer, *The Knowledge of the Holy* (San Francisco: Harper San Francisco, 1961), 154.

5 A. W. Tozer, *The Pursuit of God* (Camp Hill, Penn.: Christian Publications, 1948), 82.

6 Brennan Manning, *The Ragamuffin Gospel* (Portland, Ore.: Multnomah, 1990), 165.

7   Quoted in Calvin Miller, *Walking with Saints* (Nashville: Thomas Nelson, 1995), 121-122.

8   Quoted in Terry W. Glaspey, *Pathway to the Heart of God* (Eugene, Ore.: Harvest House, 1998), 26.

9   C. S. Lewis, *The Quotable Lewis,* ed. Wayne Martindale and Jerry Root (Wheaton, Ill.: Tyndale House Publishers, 1989), 489.

10  Eberhard Arnold, quoted in *Doubleday Christian Quotation Collection,* comp. Hannah Ward and Jennifer Wild (New York: Doubleday, 1998), 202.

11  Oswald Chambers, *Prayer: A Holy Occupation* (Grand Rapids: Discovery House Publishers, 1992), 26, 28.

12  Macarius the Elder (of Egypt c. 300-c. 390), quoted in *Doubleday Christian Quotation Collection,* comp. Hannah Ward and Jennifer Wild (New York: Doubleday, 1998), 23.

13  Henry Ward Beecher, *Treasury of the Christian Faith* (New York: Association Press, 1949), 761.

14  Catherine Marshall, *Something More* (Carmel, N.Y.: Guideposts Association, 1974), 30.

15  Georgia Harkness, *Prayer and the Common Life,* quoted in *Disciplines for the Inner Life,* by Bob Benson, Sr., and Michael W. Benson (Nashville: Thomas Nelson, 1989), 402.

16  John Cassian, quoted in Ward and Wild, *Doubleday Christian Quotation Collection,* 29.

## YOUTH

### WHAT IS MY PASSION?

1   John Powell, *A Reason to Live! A Reason to Die!* quoted in Benson and Benson, *Disciplines for the Inner Life,* 172.

2   Bernard of Clairvaux, *On Loving God,* quoted in *Spiritual Treasure:*

*Paraphrases of Spiritual Classics,* by Bernard Bangley (New York: Paulist Press, 1985), 34.

3   Margot Zilch, "May I Never Lose the Wonder" (Gospel Publishing House, 1970).

4   Oswald Chambers, *The Best of All His Books,* ed. Harry VerPloegh (Nashville: Oliver Nelson, 1989), 184.

5   Augustine, *Confessions,* described in an essay by Douglas V. Steere in *The Weavings Reader: Living with God in the World,* ed. John S. Mogabgab (Nashville: Upper Room Books, 1993), 35.

6   Quoted in Alfred E. Cooke, *Treasury of the Christian Faith* (New York: Association Press, 1949), 310.

7   Soren Kierkegaard, *For Self-Examination and Judge for Yourselves!* trans. Walter Lowrie (Princeton: Princeton University Press, 1944), 161.

8   Peter Taylor Forsyth, quoted in *Doubleday Christian Quotation Collection,* comp. Hannah Ward and Jennifer Wild (New York: Doubleday, 1998), 209.

9   Francis Thompson, *The Hound of Heaven* (Mt. Vernon, N.Y.: Peter Pauper Press, 1900).

10   Oswald Chambers, *Christian Discipline,* Vol. 2, quoted in *Disciplines for the Inner Life,* by Bob Benson, Sr., and Michael W. Benson (Nashville: Thomas Nelson, 1989), 218.

11   Andrew Murray, *Waiting on God* (London: Nisbet & Co., Ltd., 1895).

12   St. John of the Cross, quoted in *Pathway to the Heart of God,* by Terry W. Glaspey (Eugene, Ore.: Harvest House, 1998), 171.

13   Henry Blackaby and Claude V. King, *Experiencing God* (Nashville: Broadman & Holman Publishers, 1994), 217.

14   Hannah Whitall Smith, *The Christian's Secret of a Happy Life* (Old Tappan, N.J.: Fleming H. Revell Co., 1942).

15 Martin Luther, *The Table Talks of Martin Luther*, trans. William Havlitt (The Lutheran Publication Society, www.reformed.org/documents/_Table talk_2.html/).

16 Simon Tugwell, O.P., *Ways of Imperfection*, (Springfield, Ill.: Templegate Publishers, 1985), 16.

17 Adapted from Nancie Carmichael, Deeper Life column, "Knowing His Voice," *Virtue,* May/June 1994.

18 Harry Emerson Fosdick, quoted in *Treasury of the Christian Faith* (New York: Association Press, 1949).

19 Ibid., 182.

## MIDLIFE

### UNSOLVED MYSTERIES

1 Rowland P. Quilter, *The Art of Prayer* (Milwaukee: The Young Churchman Co., n.d.).

2 Calvin Miller, *If This Be Love* (New York: Harper & Row, 1984), 29.

3 John Chrysostom, quoted in *The Transforming Friendship* by James Houston (Oxford: Lion Publishing, 1989), 21.

4 Howard Thurman, *The Growing Edge*, quoted in *Disciplines for the Inner Life,* by Bob Benson, Sr., and Michael W. Benson (Nashville: Thomas Nelson, 1989), 72.

5 Thomas à Kempis, *The Imitation of Christ*, ed. Brother Leo, F. S. C. (New York: Macmillan Co., 1930).

6 George Dawson, *Little Book of Prayers*, quoted in Benson and Benson, *Disciplines for the Inner Life*, 221.

7 Henri Nouwen, *With Open Hands* (New York: Walker & Co., 1995).

8 Adapted from Nancie Carmichael, Deeper Life column, *Virtue,* April/May 1999.

9   Walter Brueggeman, *Finally Comes the Poet* (Minneapolis, Minn.: Augsburg Press, 1989), 109.

10  Walter Wangerin, Jr., *As for Me and My House* (Nashville: Thomas Nelson, 1987), 79.

11  Augustine of Hippo, quoted in *Doubleday Christian Quotation Collection*, comp. Hannah Ward and Jennifer Wild (New York: Doubleday, 1998), 28.

12  James Houston, *The Transforming Friendship* (Oxford: Lion Publishing, 1989), 243.

13  Jean Ingelow, quoted in *Lord, Bless My Child*, by William and Nancie Carmichael (Wheaton, Ill.: Tyndale House Publishers, 1995).

14  John Donne, from "Holy Sonnet XIV," *Classics of Western Spirituality*, ed. John Booty (New York: Paulist Press, 1990), 208.

15  Henri Nouwen, *The Living Reminder: Service and Prayer in Memory of Jesus Christ* (San Francisco: Harper San Francisco, 1984).

16  Oscar Wilde, "The Ballad of Reading Gaol" (1898).

17  Adapted from Nancie Carmichael, Deeper Life column, *Virtue,* January/February 1997.

18  Paul Tillich, from *The Shaking of the Foundations* (New York: Charles Scribner & Sons, 1948), 149-150.

19  John Donne, quoted in *Classics of Western Spirituality*, ed. Booty, 54.

20  Fenelon, quoted in *Spiritual Treasure: Paraphrases of Spiritual Classics,* by Bernard Bangley (New York: Paulist Press, 1985), 91.

21  Teresa of Avila, *A Life of Prayer* (Portland, Ore.: Multnomah, 1983), 25.

22  Adapted from Andrew Murray, *Waiting on God* (London: Nisbet & Co., Ltd., 1895).

## MATURITY

### EFFECTIVE PRAYERS FROM AN EFFECTIVE LIFE

1   Oswald Chambers, *The Best of All His Books,* ed. Harry VerPloegh (Nashville: Oliver Nelson, 1989), 1.

2   A. W. Tozer, *The Pursuit of God* (Camp Hill, Penn.: Christian Publications, 1948).

3   Emilie Griffin, *Homeward Voyage* (Ann Arbor, Mich.: Servant Publications, 1994), 27.

4   Dietrich Bonhoeffer, *The Cost of Discipleship,* quoted in *Doubleday Christian Quotation Collection,* comp. Hannah Ward and Jennifer Wild (New York: Doubleday, 1998), 205.

5   Henry Blackaby, *Experiencing God* (Nashville: Broadman & Holman Publishers, 1994), 107, 122.

6   Twila Paris, "Where He Leads Me" (Nashville: Myrrh Records, Word, Inc., 1995).

7   Richard Foster, *Celebration of Discipline* (New York: Harper & Row, 1978), 193.

8   Eugene H. Peterson, *Praying with Jesus* (San Francisco: Harper San Francisco, 1993).

9   Simon Schama, *Citizens: A Chronicle of the French Revolution* (New York: Alfred A. Knopf, 1989).

10  Dr. J. Edwin Orr, *Campus Aflame* (Glendale, Calif.: Regal Books, 1971).

11  Elmer Towns, *Fasting for Spiritual Breakthrough* (Glendale, Calif.: Regal Books, 1996), 17-18.

12  Adapted from Nancie Carmichael, Deeper Life column, *Virtue,* February/March 1999.

13  John Baille, in *A Diary of Private Prayer,* quoted in *Disciplines for the*

*Inner Life,* by Bob Benson, Sr., and Michael W. Benson (Nashville: Thomas Nelson, 1989), 79.

14 Joachim Neander, quoted in *The Transforming Friendship,* by James Houston (Oxford: Lion, 1989).

15 Edward King, quoted in Ward and Wild, *Doubleday Christian Quotation Collection,* 178.

16 Mrs. Hamilton King, quoted in *The Life of Joseph,* by F. B. Meyer (Lynnwood, Wash.: Emerald Books), 119.

17 J. W. Follette, *Broken Bread* (Springfield, Mo.: Gospel Publishing House, 1957), 33.

18 Blessed Elizabeth of the Trinity, *Prayers of the Women Mystics,* ed. Ronda DeSola Chervin (Ann Arbor, Mich.: Servant Publications, 1992), 207.

19 Henri Nouwen, *In the Name of Jesus* (New York: Crossroad Publishing Co., 1992), 24.

20 Madame Jeanne Guyon, *The Way Out: The study of Exodus* (Auburn, Maine: Christian Books, reprinted 1985), 62.

21 Evagrius of Pontus, quoted in Ward and Wild, *Doubleday Christian Quotation Collection,* 19-20.